D0507754

New Studies in Practical Philosophy

HAPPINESS

New Studies in Practical Philosophy

General Editor: W. D. Hudson

The point of view of this series is that
of contemporary analytical philosophy.
Each study will deal with an aspect of
moral philosophy. Particular attention
will be paid to the logic of moral discourse,
and the practical problems of morality.
The relationship between morality and
other 'universes of discourse', such as art
and science, will also be explored.

Published

R. W. Beardsmore *Art and Morality*
J. M. Brennan *The Open-Texture of Moral Concepts*
Anthony Flew *Crime or Disease?*
Anthony Flew *Sociology, Equality and Education*
R. M. Hare *Practical Inferences*
R. M. Hare *Essays on Philosophical Method*
R. M. Hare *Essays on the Moral Concepts*
R. M. Hare *Applications of Moral Philosophy*
Pamela Huby *Plato and Modern Morality*
N. M. L. Nathan *The Concept of Justice*
T. A. Roberts *The Concept of Benevolence*
Elizabeth Telfer *Happiness*

HAPPINESS

An examination of a hedonistic and a eudaemonistic concept of
happiness and of the relations between them, with a
consideration of how far and in what sense either kind of
happiness may be said to be the goal of human life.

ELIZABETH TELFER

First published 1980 by
THE MACMILLAN PRESS LTD
London and Basingstoke
Associated companies in Delhi Dublin
Hong Kong Johannesburg Lagos Melbourne
New York Singapore and Tokyo

Typeset in Great Britain by
VANTAGE PHOTOSETTING CO LTD
Southampton and London

Printed in Hong Kong

British Library Cataloguing in Publication Data

Telfer, Elizabeth
    Happiness. – (New studies in practical philosophy).
    1.   Happiness
    I.   Title   II.   Series
    128'.3   BJ1481

    ISBN 0–333–28082–2

Contents

The jacket illustration is reproduced by
permission of the Mansell Collection.

Editor's Foreword

Through the ages moral philosophers have had a great deal to say about happiness. Some of them have declared that actions are not virtuous unless they increase human happiness; and others have been equally certain that men cannot be happy unless they are virtuous. The most cursory acquaintance with all this is enough to show how varied the things meant by happiness can be and what confusions the term can conceal.

Elizabeth Telfer makes what is perhaps the most meticulous attempt in recent philosophy to clarify the concept of happiness. Her main distinction is between happiness in the hedonistic sense of being pleased with one's life and in the eudaemonistic sense of having what is worth having in life. She brings under critical scrutiny what Aristotle, Kant, Mill and others have said about our duty to pursue these kinds of happiness for ourselves and others, and explains her own opinions about the relationship between them.

W. D. HUDSON

TO ROBERT DOWNIE

1 The Nature of Happiness

It is very often maintained, both by philosophers and by
laymen, that the point or purpose of human life is to achieve
happiness, or that happiness is the *summum bonum*, or again that
it is the final or ultimate end of human activity. The purpose of
this essay is to investigate the meaning and the plausibility of
such claims.

1 *A Definition of Happiness*[1]

The first step in this process is to examine the concept of
happiness itself. And here at once I encounter a difficulty, since
there may well be different concepts referred to by the term: in
particular, the Greek idea of *eudaemonia*, normally translated by
'happiness', may not be the same in all respects as our idea of
happiness. To begin with, however, I shall try to elucidate a
modern non-technical concept employed in everyday speech,
and note possible variations on this at a later stage.

The kind of happiness I am attempting to analyse is not
however the only kind referred to, even in ordinary speech.
Thus we can, I think, distinguish a happy temperament or
disposition; a happy mood or frame of mind, 'feeling happy';
'happy' as equivalent to 'enjoyable' or 'pleasant'; and finally
what I want to call 'happiness in life'. A happy *temperament*,
often attributed to young children, is a disposition to be
cheerful, to find things agreeable. One can speak of someone as
a '*naturally* happy' person in this sense, meaning among other
things that he is likely to manage to be happy in life even in very
difficult circumstances. A happy *mood* is a (temporary) inclination to look on the bright side or find things agreeable, sometimes coupled with a recognition that in fact things are in a bad
way; like other moods, its existence can often be explained by
causes rather than reasons, in this case such things as a good

dinner. 'Happy' meaning 'enjoyable' or 'pleasant' occurs in
sentences like 'I spent a happy evening looking through old
photographs', and a similar use is that exhibited when we say of
a child paddling in the mud 'He's very happy', meaning 'He's
enjoying himself'. Happiness *in life* is the kind which is in
question when someone says, 'At last he has found happiness',
or 'I'm a very happy man', or 'The way to happiness is to have a
good bank balance, a good cook and a good digestion', or 'He
had a very happy life.' It is presumably happiness *in life* which
is the kind of happiness relevant to a discussion of aims in life; I
shall begin by considering happiness in life and then at the end
of the section ask what part the other forms of happiness play in
happiness in life.

What, then, is happiness in the sense of 'happiness in life'? It
is often connected, as by Aristotle, with the achievement of
one's major goals: things towards which a man directs his
activities. Thus Aristotle says that to find out how a man
conceives of happiness we have only to look at what he aims at
in life: honour, wealth, or whatever it may be.[2] Aristotle seems
to assume that a man must have some *one* aim in life to which
everything else is subordinated; but there seems no reason why
a man should not have *several* such aims, no one of which is
subordinated to any other: 'What I'm aiming for in life is a
worthwhile job, a happy marriage and beautiful surroundings
to live in.'

It is sometimes suggested that a man's basic aims must be
integrated in some way into a *pattern*. If this is a logical 'must',
however, it seems to be false: what pattern is formed by the
items I have mentioned? Nor is it clear that there is any
psychological necessity to have an order of priority established
among one's goals: circumstances might force a decision on
priorities on a given occasion, but such decisions need not form
a consistent pattern. What might be meant is the 'must' of
practical advice: in working for several aims the most successful
course will be to establish an order of priorities and try to
integrate one's pursuit: for example, to look for a worthwhile
job which will itself require that one lives in beautiful surroundings. This is probably good advice. But there are plenty of
people who work for several aims in a muddled and conflicting
manner and still achieve them through luck; so whereas it may

be that a man must integrate his aims to be sensible, it need not be the case that a man must integrate his aims to be successful.

Now a man can certainly give as his reason for being happy the fact that he has achieved his major aims: 'I'm a happy man – I've achieved all the things I've been working for in life.' As with my example, these aims may well include things which cannot be achieved once and for all: it would often be appropriate to say, 'I am so far achieving my aim of a happy marriage.' Again, a man may be made happy by the *prospect* of achieving his aim, before it is actually won: 'I'm very happy – I'm training to be a doctor, which is the only thing I ever wanted to be.'

The suggestion then is that the achievement of one's major aims is a necessary condition of happiness, in the sense that someone who has major aims in life but who is unable to achieve them will not be happy. I am not including a person who *gives up* an aim, either deliberately or not; in such a case we would not say that he *has* aims which he is not achieving. Nor am I to be taken as saying that a person who *has* no aims in life (and so *a fortiori* does not fulfil them) is not happy. I am saying only that if someone does have major aims in life he will not be happy while the achievement of these is frustrated. This is not necessarily to say that he will be *un*happy: a man can perfectly well say 'If I can achieve such-and-such I shall be happy', without being ready to say that he is at present unhappy.

It should be noted that in speaking of the achievement of aims as a necessary condition of happiness, I have not specified whether it is to be regarded as logically or causally necessary; it may turn out that such achievement is part of what constitutes happiness, or alternatively it may be that it produces or arouses an attitude or state of mind which is to be identified with happiness. I shall turn to an examination of this question when I have considered other suggested necessary conditions for happiness.

For to have achieved, to be achieving or to be on the way to achieving one's aims, even if necessary, is not by itself a sufficient condition for happiness. Happiness may be spoilt, even when this condition is met, by some major misfortune or disability or cause of distress or pain: 'I've got everything I ever worked for, but I can't be happy because I'm so ugly.' We have then two necessary conditions for happiness: achievement of major aims and freedom from major distresses.

It might now be said that the second condition can be subsumed under the first, on the grounds that one of a man's aims in life must surely be to achieve freedom from his distresses. This will indeed be so where the affliction is of a type about which something can be done. But very often, as in my example, nothing *can* be done, or at least it may seem to the sufferer that nothing can be done. It will not make sense to say that someone *aims* at becoming less ugly, since to aim at something is to take steps towards achieving it; the most one can say is that he *wishes* he were less ugly. Afflictions range from those which the sufferers are bending every effort to remove – here we *can* of course say that the removal of the affliction is a major aim – through those which they hope will pass one day of themselves, to those which they wish they could lose but despair of ever doing so. We can unify this whole range, however, by abandoning the concept of an aim in favour of the weaker concept of wanting: thus we can say that happiness requires that there be nothing major in one's life which one wants very much to have otherwise.

A word is needed here about the notion of a *major* aim or a *major* affliction. It is clear that not every trivial frustration or mishap makes a person unhappy. But what counts as trivial or major depends, not on the situation itself, but on how it is *viewed*; what is trivial to one person is major to another. The difficulty then is to define 'major' without using the idea of happiness in the definition, and saying in effect '"Major" means "important enough to affect happiness"'. But this circularity can be avoided if we give an account in terms of the degree of *attention* paid to the frustration or affliction: the degree to which the sufferer broods on it, talks about it, and so on.

It might now be objected that there are stoical characters who will not allow themselves to dwell on frustrations or misfortunes, and that my definition of 'major' turns all the troubles of such people into minor ones. But in fact the case of the stoic can be accommodated without depriving him of major frustrations or misfortunes in this way. In some cases he will indeed succeed in converting what might have been a major disaster into a minor one, by confining its impact through his stoicism. But in other cases a frustration or misfortune can be said to be major for him, despite his refusal consciously to dwell on it, in that it interferes with other aspects of his life: for example, it may interfere with the pursuit of other aims by causing the sufferer to 'lose heart' for everything. We can therefore define a major frustration or affliction as one which receives a lot of attention from the sufferer, while noting that this may either be voluntarily paid by him or exacted from him despite himself in the form of interference with his life.

So far we have a rather asymmetrical picture of necessary conditions for happiness; on the positive side we have the achievement of *goals*, whereas on the negative side we have the absence of anything major which one *wants* to be otherwise, whether this wanting amounts to the pursuit of a goal or not. This mention of goals came about because we started from the Aristotelian notion of happiness as involving goals pursued. But I think that on the positive no less than the negative side it would be better to widen the scope to include the achievement of everything important which is *wanted*, whether or not it is made into a goal. For a man may describe his happiness as arising from things which he wanted but did not pursue as goals – perhaps because they cannot be pursued, or because he thinks they cannot or should not be. Thus someone might say, 'I'm happy – I've got what I always wanted – a marriage with someone whom I can regard as a second self and who shares all my pursuits at work and leisure.' But he might be indignant at the idea that such a marriage had been a *goal* which he pursued, feeling that such things have to be left to providence. Again, a girl might very much want to be 'swept off her feet' by Mr Right appearing out of the blue, and want this in such a way that part of what she wants is precisely not to *do* anything about it.

We arrive, then, at a schematic account of the happy man, as one who has everything major which he wanted and has nothing major which he wishes were otherwise; with due allowance for the points I made earlier, about happiness sometimes arising from the prospect of success rather than its fullblown achievement, and about some goals being by nature achieved continuously rather than all at once. Is this a complete account of the conditions of happiness? In other words, are these conditions not only necessary but jointly sufficient? I think we must say no, because I have not taken account of the fact that there are *two* ways of failing to achieve happiness with regard to what we want: not only can people have unfulfilled desires which prevent their happiness, but also they can fail to achieve happiness because they get what they want and then do not like it. This is not just a minor point: fairy tale, myth and fiction, as well as real life, are full of stories about people who wanted something very much but found when they had it that it made them miserable rather than happy, and this possibility is central to our thinking about happiness.

It may however be objected that if a person is disappointed with what he gets, this shows that he did not really want it – he only thought he did; and that conversely if a person is unexpectedly pleased with what he gets, this shows that he really wanted it all the time. Now it is true that we do *say* of someone who is disappointed that he did not really want what he has got. But this is not the same sense of 'want' as that which we have been using hitherto. In that sense, which implies striving to get where possible and a conscious hope of attainment or at least a wish, a person can certainly want something which he subsequently does not like.

Of course there are cases of self-deception, where a person pretends to himself that he wants something which he thinks it creditable to want, or which other people want him to want. In these situations it *is* proper to say that he did not really want what he pretended to want. But in such a case he can come, or be brought, to a realisation that he is not sincere, *before* he achieves what he is supposed to want: for example, by acknowledging the relief he feels when what he is supposed to want becomes impossible. What I am talking about, however, is the case where someone is perfectly sincere in wanting what eventually proves disappointing. There are therefore *two* senses of the phrase 'really wants': it can mean either 'actually wants' (in a conative, hoping and striving sense of 'want') as opposed to 'pretends to want', 'is said to want', and so on; or it can mean 'will/would be pleased with'. A person can really want something in either of these senses without really wanting it in the other. I shall henceforward use inverted commas round the phrase when using it in the second sense. Note that to say someone 'really wants' something is ostensibly to speak of his future rather than of his present state of mind. It might be claimed that there must logically be something about a person *now* – a propensity or leaning or tendency or taste or whatever – by virtue of which he will be pleased with a thing in the future. This is probably so, but it does not affect my present point.

Of course people can often give *reasons* for being disappointed with what they wanted: 'I wanted to be a lecturer because I thought it would be an easy life, but I find it's a fearful struggle, so I'm disappointed.' Because of this, the tempting move, in considering cases where people want things which later prove disappointing, is to say that what was wanted was not the thing itself but some feature or character which it was thought to have but which it turned out not to possess; in this example, 'an easy life'. On this analysis the person's situation is *not* accurately described by saying that he got what he had wanted but was disappointed, since he did *not* get precisely what he had wanted.

But I think this move should be resisted. For one thing, there is a perfectly normal sense in which the wanter *did* want what he said he wanted; if the fact that he wanted it for reasons shows that he did not want *it*, it becomes impossible to want anything except for its own sake. Secondly, there are not always features which the disappointed wanter can point to the absence of – he may not know why he is disappointed. Thirdly, we cannot on this kind of view fit in the person who is unexpectedly *pleased*: what did *he* want? I insist then that one can be said to want a thing and be disappointed with it, and conversely be pleased with something which one did not previously want.

I do not wish to exaggerate the frequency of this discrepancy between people's wants and their eventual reaction to getting what they previously wanted; often, of course, people do 'know what they want', in the sense of knowing what they 'really want', what will please them. But if we are to give due weight to the occasional occurrence of these discrepancies, we cannot simply speak of getting what one wanted as a necessary condition of happiness. Instead we shall need to use the notion I have already employed, of being *pleased* with what one gets. The happy man, then, is one who is *pleased* with what he gets in life. This is very often what he previously wanted, though he *may* fail to be pleased with that. But it is possible also to be pleased with

unexpected things, even with things which one did *not* originally want, and associate them with one's happiness: 'When I
was a student the last thing I wanted was to be a teacher, and
getting married was almost as bad in my view. But now here am
I, married and a teacher – and I'm very happy.'

It might however be said that the concept of being pleased is
too near to that of happiness to provide an illuminating *analy-
sans* of it. To get round this difficulty, I suggest that being
pleased is itself to be analysed in terms of wanting – not *previous*
wants, but the *present* state of wanting to hang on to what one
has. A person who is pleased with something seeks to cherish it
and wards off interference with it. He wants to have it as it is.
With this in mind, I lay down necessary conditions for happiness as follows: a happy man does not want anything major in
his life to be otherwise; he is pleased with, that is wants (to
keep), what he has got; there is nothing major which he has not
got and which he wants (to get).

But these conditions are still not *sufficient* for happiness, since
we can imagine someone who fulfilled all these conditions still
being unhappy. That is, he might be prepared to say that there
is no great sorrow in his life, that there is nothing which he
wants but has not got, that he is pleased with all the various
items which make up his life, but still insist that something is
wrong. What this amounts to is that he wants his life to be
different in some way, without being able to say in what way: in
other words, although he is pleased with various aspects *in* his
life, he is not pleased with his *life*. This kind of case brings out
the point that happiness (or unhappiness, as in this case)
involves life viewed as a *whole*. The same situation could be
illustrated in the case of being pleased with some more specific
thing, one's spouse, say. Necessary conditions for this would be
finding nothing very important wrong with him or her, liking
the important aspects of his or her personality, not wishing that
he or she had some trait which he or she does not have. But
these are not sufficient, since a person might still not be pleased
with a spouse without being able to say what was amiss; to state
a *sufficient* condition, therefore, one could say only 'I want to
have him or her as he or she is'.

My suggestion for a definition of happiness, then, is that it is
a state of being pleased with one's life as a whole: a state for

which the conditions I mentioned earlier, that there is nothing one wants but has not got, and so on, are necessary but not sufficient conditions. I think moreover that it is now clear that the necessity in question is a logical or conceptual, rather than a causal, necessity. It is not a contingency that in order to be pleased with a thing one must find nothing major wrong with it, welcome its positive features and so on. On the other hand, it *is* presumably a contingent matter, to do with human nature in general or a particular individual's temperament, that specific things 'make' a person happy or unhappy: that, for example, he is pleased to have a demanding job, or dissatisfied because he has not much money.

It will be noted that I have defined happiness as some kind of *attitude* of mind. Three consequences of importance flow from this. Firstly, it is on my account a category mistake to say that happiness *consists* in the acquisition of wealth, or the pursuit of knowledge, or the exercise of virtue, or in any combination of things which are not attitudes. It may be that happiness is causally *produced* by or *dependent* on some list of particular things, or even that there is only one thing necessary to make everyone pleased with life. But on my view to say happiness *is* for example contemplation can only be shorthand for saying that human beings are made happy by or find happiness in a life of contemplation.

Secondly, my analysis entails that, broadly speaking at least, a man is himself the authority on whether or not he is happy. Other people may say, 'You've got this and that – you *ought* to be happy' – meaning either 'We would expect you to be happy', or 'A person of sound attitudes would in your position be happy' – but if he insists that he is not, they are in no position to refute him. Of course other people may be better judges than the man himself of what will make him happy or unhappy in the future, just as someone else may be a better judge than oneself of whether one will enjoy some experience: 'You'll enjoy your examinations once you begin' can turn out to be true.

It is sometimes maintained that there are kinds of case where one person can meaningfully say of another 'He is not "really" happy', although he himself insists that he is: for example, the drug addict who has a plentiful supply of his drug may call himself happy although others are reluctant to call him so.[3]

This reluctance need not however constitute a difficulty for my analysis. It may for example be due to a reluctance to believe in the sincerity of the addict, a tendency to think that he must be indulging in some kind of self-deception because no one could really be pleased with such a life.

If however it is admitted that the drug addict *is* pleased with his life but claimed that he is for all that not *happy*, my reply is that this is a different sense of 'happy' from that which I have been elucidating. The speaker wishes to add to the notion of being pleased with life, or to substitute for it, the notion of being fortunate or enviable, or alternatively that of being admirable: since the drug addict is not fortunate (or not admirable) he is not happy.

I do not wish to deny the importance of the ideas of the fortunate and the admirable, nor that it may be possible to use the word 'happy' in such a connection. But my present concern is to analyse the perfectly valid use of the term which does *not* carry the necessary implication of a way of life which is fortunate or admirable: thus, in my usage one can say, 'She has a life which most people would find awful, but she is perfectly happy', or 'He has wasted his life and prostituted his talents, and what's more, he's perfectly happy.'

The third consequence of the 'attitudinal' nature of happiness is that a person who is unhappy can become happy in either of two ways: by altering his circumstances or by altering his attitude to his circumstances. For example, a person who is unhappy because he is unpopular can become happy either by becoming popular, or by ceasing to care about being unpopular. The successful stoic whom I mentioned earlier, who succeeds in genuinely minimising the effect of a misfortune, is one example of the achievement of happiness by the latter process. It need not be an admirable process; thus the drug addict I mentioned earlier has achieved happiness by reducing his horizons till there is only one thing he cares about in life, and provided he gets that he is happy.

I shall now return to the three forms of happiness, distinguished from 'happiness in life', which I mentioned at the beginning of the section: a happy temperament, feeling happy and having a happy time. Can we now see what part these play in happiness proper? A happy temperament can be dealt with fairly briefly in the light of the point I have just made about adjusting attitudes: presumably such a temperament is one which suits its wishes to the circumstances more readily than average. There are perhaps attractive and unattractive aspects to the happy temperament: it is realistic and free from pigheadedness, but also relatively unambitious and perhaps complacent.

The happiness of a happy mood raises the question whether the relationship between it and happiness in life is really only one of degree: is happiness in life really only a longer-lasting mood of happiness? I think that the distinction can be shown to be one of kind and not merely of degree, for many reasons, some of which need a little discussion. The first reason is that happiness in life, unlike a happy mood, seems to require reasons rather than causes to explain it: it is perfectly comprehensible to say 'I feel happy this evening, I don't know why – it must be the good dinner', but *not* equally comprehensible to say 'I'm a happy man, I don't know why.' Such a man will be expected to be able to enumerate at least some of the things which please him in his life.

The second reason is that a happy mood is, as we saw earlier, compatible with a recognition that things are not in fact as one wants them: thus one can say, 'I'm *feeling* happy this evening', or 'I'm *feeling* pleased with life', while at the same time being unwilling to say, as being happy would require, that one really *is* pleased with one's life.

The third reason is that a happy mood is something of which its possessor is necessarily aware, since it colours the way everything is seen; whereas happiness is something a man may possess without necessarily being aware of it. What I mean by this is that if asked whether he is happy he may need to stop and think, and survey and assess his life, before coming to a decision. Of course, this need not be the case; a person who is 'blissfully happy' will be made aware of his happiness by various emotions. But I would maintain that happiness *need* not be an emotional business, at least in the sense of a psychologically and physically disturbing business: a person can come to realise he is happy in much the same way as he can come to realise he is pleased with something specific, by realising (perhaps only when it is threatened) how much he wants to keep his way of life as it is.

Before leaving the subject of the happy mood, I should like to

challenge the idea that happiness in life necessarily differs from
the happy mood in duration, as well as in these other ways. It is
a commonplace philosophical idea that happiness differs from
pleasure, for example, in being relatively *long-lasting*. But the
way I have defined it does not make this necessary, though it
will certainly be usual. Consider, for example, a girl made
unhappy by the belief that the man she adores does not care for
her, made happy by his declaration that he loves her, and made
unhappy again by his death; the period of the happiness might
in this case be only a day or so. But during this time the girl
would be, and say that she is, entirely pleased with her life.

Of course if someone *foresees* an imminent misfortune he will
probably not be completely happy. To be pleased with one's life
involves for most people being pleased with one's prospects; in
that sense happiness does have a long-term reference, the
length of the period presumably varying with the person, in
that some people 'live in the present' more than others. But the
Greek idea 'count no man happy until he is dead'[4] – meaning
that he cannot be deemed to be happy until beyond the reach of
any possibility of calamity – applies rather to the idea of good
fortune than to the conception of happiness I have been
outlining. It is true that one cannot speak of someone's having
had a happy *life*, even in my sense of 'happy', until the whole life
span can be surveyed. But this is not to say that a person may
not possess happiness 'in life' for a day, since 'in life' here refers
not to a time-span but to the all-embracing scope of happiness.

The third kind of happiness referred to at the beginning of
this chapter was 'having a happy time', which, as I said earlier,
is roughly equivalent to enjoying oneself. Now enjoyment is
equivalent to, or is a form of, *pleasure*, and so what seems to be in
question here is the relationship between pleasure and happiness. Any attempt to give an account of the nature of happiness
clearly must grapple with this topic.

2   *Pleasure and Happiness*

Something has already been said about pleasure and happiness, since in analysing happiness I have spoken a good deal of
being pleased, which is also presumably a form of pleasure; so I
shall need to consider how enjoyment differs from being

pleased if I am to connect the concept of enjoyment or 'having a happy time' with the analysis of happiness so far given. But first let me give a very rough and ready account of pleasure in general.

The concept of pleasure is notoriously difficult to analyse, and I shall not do more than give a few indications. I think it is clear that pleasure is not a physical *sensation* (though 'pain' can mean a physical sensation, and there can be sensations which *give* pleasure, and there can be sensations associated with pleasure, glows of satisfaction and so forth); it is also clear that it is not a *mood*. We are told by Ryle that it is not an emotion either, but of this I am less convinced.[5] It is true that emotions typically involve turmoil and disruption, while pleasure typically does not; but then pleasure *can* be a disrupting thing, in the manner of an emotion ('transports of delight', for example) and emotions, or at any rate something akin to them, need not be: 'I was rather annoyed when he said that' can be an expression of a reaction which, although perhaps a species of anger, does not confuse the train of thought or heighten the colour.

If I were to try to classify pleasure, it would be with the emotions, and perhaps especially with that milder aspect of them which we might term reactions or responses. For longer-term cases, 'attitude' might be the more appropriate word: 'What is your attitude to your daughter's success as a strip-tease artist?' 'I'm very pleased about it.' In classing pleasure with emotions and attitudes, I am acknowledging that it carries with it *conative* implications, of how the person who gets pleasure from something will tend to act towards that thing. As I have already argued, the man who is pleased with something wants to hang on to it, cherish it, keep it as it is. Similarly the man who is enjoying something wants it to go on, or at least wants it not to be interrupted. As may be already clear from my remarks about being pleased in the context of the analysis of happiness, I think that the desires with which pleasure is necessarily connected are those which obtain when the object of pleasure is acquired, rather than those felt in advance of achieving it, since it is possible to want something and then not get pleasure from attaining it.

Enjoyment and being pleased can, however, be distinguished: first of all by the scope of their *objects*, that which a man may be said to enjoy or to be pleased at, with or by. Thus one can be said to be *pleased* by almost any kind of thing: the result of the General Election, one's own success in keeping one's temper in trying circumstances, a new dress, the government's stand on pornography. On the other hand one can be said to *enjoy* only one's own activities or experiences: playing tennis, studying philosophy, sunbathing, being tickled. Apparent counter-examples, in which other categories of thing are said to be enjoyed, can all in the end be brought under this formula: thus to enjoy an object, such as a book, is to enjoy *reading* it, to enjoy another's experiences such as a friend's fame (as distinct from being pleased by it) is to bask in the reflected glory which it gives oneself, and so on.

A second difference is in the kinds of *reason* which can be given in each case. One can be pleased with something not because of anything in its own nature but because it fits in with some goal or wish fairly remotely connected with it, whereas reasons for enjoyment can only be in terms of further specification of the enjoyed thing itself. For example, I can be pleased to have read a book because I want to be able to say I have done so at parties; but I cannot be said to *enjoy* it for that reason, but only for such things as the character-drawing, the style of writing, and so on. Of course, I can, while reading the book, enjoy imagining my success at the next cocktail party – but this is not the same as enjoying the book.

A third difference between being pleased and enjoyment which is sometimes suggested is that one is pleased when one achieves what one wanted, what will be conducive to what one wanted, what is a part of what one wanted, and so on; whereas (it is said) enjoyment is not dependent on previous wants at all. Now there is certainly some difference along these lines, but its nature is not quite what has been made out. As we have already seen, one can be pleased by something which formed no part of one's world of wants. As a further example of this, consider the earnest supporter of Women's Liberation who finds that she is pleased by some old-fashioned compliment, but would indignantly and quite sincerely deny that this was the kind of thing she *wanted*. As we saw, it is open to someone to say that this incident just showed that there was a sense in which she wanted

compliments 'all along'. But a necessary connection with wanting in this sense, what I called 'really wanting', will not
distinguish being pleased from enjoyment. For in the 'really
wanting' sense of wanting people also *enjoy* only those things
which they wanted: it might in the same way be said of someone
who thought he would hate studying philosophy, but finally
enjoyed it, that he must have wanted this, or this sort of thing,
all along.

The difference between being pleased and enjoyment in
respect of previous wants, then, is not really that being pleased
is dependent on previous wants while enjoyment is not. It
depends on the fact that being pleased is a *wider* notion than
enjoyment, covering not only a reaction to things 'in themselves' but also a reaction to things because of their possible
results, concomitants, and so on; we saw this in connection with
the kinds of reason which can be given for being pleased. Where
I am pleased with something for a reason of this kind, then, my
pleasure does, by definition, depend on a previous (and still
existing) want: I am pleased with X because I want Y and I
think X will lead to Y. Note that the want on which being
pleased for a reason depends is not a want for the thing with
which I am pleased: I am pleased with X because I wanted Y. I
may or may not, according to the circumstances, have wanted
X itself; I may be pleased that someone is going to America
because I want never to see him again, but I probably did not
want him *to go to America* as such, unless this had presented itself
as a possible solution to my problem. Where I am pleased with
something, but not for a reason of this kind, there is no necessity
for a previous want at all: I can be pleased by a compliment
without having wanted one, or I can be pleased by a compliment
having wanted one. Being pleased is in this respect like enjoyment: I can enjoy skiing having wanted to go skiing or I can
enjoy it not having wanted it.

I can now suggest an account of the relationship between
being pleased and enjoyment. Both being pleased and enjoyment are subspecies of pleasure, enjoyment comprising only
those cases of pleasure where the object (that which pleases)
not only does so by virtue of its own nature rather than its
consequences, but also is an experience or activity of him whose
pleasure is in question, being pleased comprising all the rest. If

it were idiomatic to say, 'Are you being pleased by that?' as an equivalent to 'Are you enjoying it?', one might say that being pleased was simply a synonym for 'being given pleasure' and enjoyment therefore a subspecies of being pleased. But it does not seem possible to use 'being pleased' in this continuous way in English: hence the enjoyment cases are cases of pleasure which are not also cases of being pleased.

After this excursus on the nature of pleasure, I turn finally to the relationship between pleasure and happiness. As we have seen, pleasure in the sense of being pleased is firmly built into my analysis of happiness. But those who consider the question of the relationship between pleasure and happiness often have in mind enjoyment in particular; and indeed my point of departure for this discussion of pleasure was the relationship between 'having a happy afternoon', which meant 'enjoying oneself for the afternoon', and happiness proper. So the question now arises as to the part *enjoyment*, as distinct from pleasure in general, plays in happiness. On my analysis this question can be posed in its sharpest form as follows: can people be pleased with a life which has no enjoyment in it? When the question is put like this the answer seems to be: most cannot, but some can. For example, one can imagine some austere scientist who was pleased with his life because he was achieving great increases in human knowledge and who wanted nothing else from life; and who refused to describe himself as enjoying practising science, or enjoying doing anything else in his life either. Could this not be a kind of happiness? This is of course an extreme case, but there are many people for whom achievements matter more than enjoyments, and who will be pleased with a life with few enjoyments if it includes many achievements.

Of course the life of achievement will typically bring with it some enjoyment; for example, a scientist usually enjoys much of his work, and whereas he may not set conscious store by this enjoyment, its absence might be the kind of thing which made him say, 'There's something missing in my life – I don't know what it is'. And for most people enjoyment will play a bigger and more conscious part in happiness: for example, they will be pleased with their lives partly on the grounds that they enjoy their work and have leisure pursuits which they also enjoy; or they will fail to be happy because they do not enjoy their work, and any achievements they may win in it fail to compensate for this. Or again a person who is not happy may survey his life and say, 'Everything is drab – I never seem to be able to enjoy myself', and give this as the reason why he is not happy. It seems then that for many people, though not all, 'having a happy time' now and again is necessary for happiness.

There are also people who think that enjoyment, even if not necessary for everyone's happiness, is sufficient for it: that anyone will be happy provided he can spend all his time doing things he enjoys. Here, however, we must distinguish two different cases. The first case is that of the person who enjoys almost all the things he does, including a great many things of which the point is not enjoyment at all, and even those which many people do not enjoy: he enjoys his work, but he also enjoys travelling to work; he enjoys his food, but he also enjoys cooking it *and* washing up after it, and so on. While it is doubtless not possible to enjoy *everything* one does, it is possible for some people to enjoy most things they do. These are the people who are said to 'enjoy life'. The other case of a life of constant enjoyment is that which most readily springs to mind when the relationship between pleasure and happiness is in question: the life for example of the millionaire cruising on his yacht who, according to popular belief, spends his time in eating and drinking well, sight-seeing, sports and socialising, the life of what Aristotle called 'amusements'.

Is a life of enjoyment, of either of these kinds, sufficient for happiness? The prior question may be whether the second kind, the life of an Onassis, is even a life of constant *enjoyment*: surely, one is tempted to say, it must be very boring? But let us waive that difficulty. It is clear that a life of enjoyment is not sufficient for happiness in every case; for a man might be said to enjoy life, in either of these ways, and yet not be really happy, because there are specific things he wants but does not have: for example, children. But perhaps it might be sufficient for some people's happiness: that is, they might be pleased with their lives and feel that they lack nothing, solely because they enjoy themselves all or most of the time.

The problem here, however, is to imagine what a pure case of such happiness would be like. At least in the first case of the life of enjoyment, the man's happiness would in practice depend,

not only on his enjoyment, but also on other satisfactions: he
will for example be pleased that he is doing a useful job, pleased
that his children are turning out well, and so on. And indeed it
is difficult to imagine a life, however sybaritic, that did not
include pleasures of this kind that are not those of enjoyment.
Even the 'amusements' themselves may yield pleasures that are
not those of enjoyment: for example, a well-dressed woman
may not only enjoy wearing beautiful clothes but also be
pleased (rightly or wrongly, that is not at issue here) to think
that she is by her way of life contributing to the beauty of the
world. Whether there could be a person so pig-like as to be
happy simply because he leads a life of enjoyment is partly an
empirical question (could someone be so entirely indifferent to
the considerations which bring or withhold other pleasures?),
and partly a conceptual one (would such a creature be rightly
called a person?).

From the foregoing discussion of happiness and pleasure it
will be seen that my conception of happiness is a *hedonistic*
conception, in one sense of that term. But in so far as I have cast
doubt on the centrality of enjoyment, as distinct from being
pleased, in the idea of happiness, I have I hope rescued the idea
of a hedonistic conception of happiness from some of its more
mistaken and hostile connotations.

3   *Happiness as the Only Final End*

The claim that happiness is in some sense a, or the, appropriate
final end for man is refuted *ab initio* if either of two other claims,
both of which have been advanced, can be sustained: that man
necessarily does in any case pursue only happiness as a final
end, and that man logically *cannot* pursue his own happiness. If
either of these theses were true, it would become meaningless to
say that happiness is an appropriate end; for this is to recommend its adoption as an end, and one cannot recommend that a
person should do either what he necessarily does or what he
necessarily cannot do. I shall attempt to refute both these
claims, and in this section I shall consider the claim that
happiness is necessarily our final goal, the one thing for the sake
of which, in the last analysis, everything else is done.

One philosopher who sometimes argued that this was so was

John Stuart Mill. His argument was based on an account of happiness as consisting of an aggregate of all the things a person pursues for their own sakes. He maintained that it followed from this account that everything a man seeks is sought either as part of or as a means to his happiness.[6] Now if I am right in my definition of happiness, Mill is doubly wrong in his account of its nature: firstly, he sees it as consisting in things themselves, such as wealth or virtue, rather than in an attitude to these things; secondly, he does not allow for the fact that people can get what they wanted but not be happy. His argument then does nothing to show that *my* kind of happiness is a necessary end for all.

But it seems to me that even in terms of his own account Mill's conclusion does not follow from his premise. If happiness is equivalent to an aggregate of everything sought for its own sake, it indeed follows that everything a man seeks for its own sake is in fact part of his happiness, and that everything sought as a means is thought to be a means to what is in fact part of his happiness. But it does not follow that everything a man seeks for its own sake is *sought as* part of his happiness: that is to say, seen *as* one item in a wider whole. Only if that were the case could one say that everyone necessarily seeks only happiness.

It might perhaps be said here that I am pushing the notion of happiness as an *aggregate* harder than Mill's wording really justifies; and that all Mill means is that 'happiness' is a term that can be applied jointly or severally to everything one wants, rather as the term 'property' can be applied to everything one owns. But if this is what Mill means, then there is no longer any *one* thing called happiness for the sake of which things are done; and indeed to say that things are wanted as part of one's happiness becomes as otiose as to say that things are owned as part of one's property.

Aristotle is another philosopher to whom the thesis that we necessarily seek only happiness as a final goal is attributed. At first sight his argument seems to be as follows: everything aims at some good, everyone must have final aims (or we would go on for ever), the final aim is therefore the final good; this is what is known as happiness.[7] This account looks like Mill's account of happiness, as consisting of whatever we want for its own sake, and would be open to the same criticisms. But Aristotle's story is really much more complex. For one thing, he seems to connect happiness with a *single* aim (such as honour or virtue or pleasure) for each man. If he thinks that the necessity of our having final aims *entails* the necessity of some one final aim, his reasoning is fallacious, as has often been pointed out. But he may either think for other reasons that each man must have some one final aim, or hold that only in those cases where a man does have some one final aim is it appropriate to speak of happiness. I shall say a little on each of these points.

The first proposition seems at first sight obviously false: surely a man can aim at both virtue and knowledge, or at both virtue and power, for their own sakes? Aristotle might however reply that this is by no means so obvious. Suppose a man to have several final aims in his life: what will happen if the two come into conflict? Must not there be some ranking of aims, some idea of which would be sacrificed if one had to go? If so, one of his apparent final aims is what may be called his *preferred* final aim; and this, it may be said, is the man's *most* final, or *the* final aim.

But a preferred aim is not really the same as a single final aim. To say that all other things would if necessary be sacrificed for it is not to say that they are not pursued for their own sakes, that they are pursued as means. In any case, as I have already argued, a man who has several final aims in life does not necessarily have one to which he would give preference in cases of conflict. He might be inconsistent and give preference now to one aim, now to the other. For example, a man seeking both virtue and popularity may find they conflict, and pursue a muddled way of life sacrificing now one, now the other. If Aristotle is construed as saying that each man necessarily seeks happiness in this special sense, namely that each man necessarily has some one final end in which his happiness consists, then his thesis is false.

It might be said here that a really sensible or rational man does not behave like the man I have just described; he integrates his final aims into some kind of concerted plan and decides in advance what would happen in cases of conflict; in other words, he decides what his preferred aim is. One might then *define* 'happiness' stipulatively in terms of such a worked-out hierarchy of final aims, rather than simply as Mill does as a conglomeration of aims, or as a single aim. Aristotle in the *Eudemian Ethics* seems to adopt an account more like this.[8] But, as I have said, one could not argue that everyone is rational enough to aim at happiness in *this* sense, and indeed Aristotle in the *Eudemian Ethics* concedes that people do not, as he *recommends* the adoption of this policy.

One point in Aristotle's account that I have not so far noted is that Aristotle says that people can be *wrong* about what their happiness consists in.[9] This point, taken in itself, suggests a reference to the fact that we have noted earlier, that people can get what they wanted and not be pleased with it – they no longer want it, as we say. What they are mistaken about is what they 'really want' – what they would be pleased with if they actually got it. *If* this is what Aristotle means (and I shall suggest in chapter 2 that Aristotle is in fact working with a rather different conception from the notion of happiness at present under discussion), then happiness consists in what a man 'really wants', and the thesis is that whenever he aims at things he necessarily thinks, rightly or wrongly, that they are, or will lead to, what he 'really wants' and so that they constitute his happiness or the means to it.

This view would be an improvement on Mill's, in that it makes room for the fact that a man can be mistaken about how to gain happiness. But more fundamentally, this kind of view in effect recognises that the pursuit of happiness is really the pursuit of a particular kind of *attitude*, as on my analysis it must be. For it embodies the idea that anything is part of happiness if it is 'really wanted' – in other words, it is the *attitude* which counts, rather than the thing itself. On this view, pursuing something 'for its own sake' is construed as pursuing it for the sake of one's expected attitude to it – since on this view one would not pursue a thing if one did not believe it would please when achieved.

This theory is of course a version of that known as psychological hedonism. Psychological hedonism is normally dismissed quite briskly, on the grounds that pleasure is a result of getting what was wanted for its own sake and so cannot *be* what was wanted for its own sake. As will already be clear, I think this argument inadequate as it stands, since in my view pleasure in a thing connects, not with having wanted it before, but with wanting to hang on to it. I shall argue shortly that there is no logical inconsistency in desiring pleasure for its own sake. I should in fact oppose psychological hedonism on other grounds, which will emerge shortly. But in any case the version of psychological hedonism under discussion could not support a thesis that everyone necessarily aims only at *happiness*, since it dissolves happiness into a number of separate *pleasures*. To aim at something 'for the sake of happiness' surely cannot amount simply to aiming at it because one thinks that it will be pleasing in *itself*. It must at least mean that one sees it as part of some kind of *whole*.

It might now be granted that to aim at happiness must be to aim at being pleased with one's life as a whole, rather than with separate items in it; and maintained that everyone's sole final aim is to achieve *this* state. But there seem to be many counter-examples to such a view. For example, a man may consciously reject the idea of trying to achieve a position in which he is pleased with every aspect of his life, because he thinks that for him part of what makes life worth living is having something to strive for.[10] Secondly, a man may perform actions, such as clicking a stick along a row of railings, 'just because he feels like it', with no further end in view at all. Thirdly, a man may do something for the sake of some narrow and specific end which he regards in isolation without relating it to any wider context: for example, he takes driving lessons so that he will be able to pass the driving test, without any particular idea of why he wants to pass the driving test.

The proponents of the thesis that happiness is necessarily the only final goal might try to deal with these counter-examples as follows. Firstly, they would remind us that happiness is to be construed as being pleased, not with every item *in* one's life, but with one's life as a whole; and the latter is quite consistent, as we saw earlier, with the possibility that for some people life as a whole will not please unless there are aspects of it which constitute quests rather than satisfactions. Secondly, they would discount those actions which are done 'just because one feels like it' by reformulating their basic thesis in narrower and if you like weaker terms, thus: that every action that is *calculated* or *deliberated* upon must be done for the sake of happiness, in the sense of being pleased with one's life. Thirdly, they will explain that their view need not entail that happiness is always pursued consciously and as such in every deliberated action. The thesis that everything is done for the sake of happiness should rather be construed as stating a governing principle in *conformity* with which every deliberate action is done. In other words, the thesis is that no one ever pursues a policy which he thinks will be *contrary* to his happiness.

But even this thesis is implausible. There are many apparent counter-examples, of which I shall mention four types: (i) a man may quite knowingly and deliberately sacrifice his happiness to pursue revenge, or to marry a girl with whom he is infatuated but with whom he sees he can never be happy; (ii) a man may think that he can achieve happiness only by doing something he considers wrong, and so he may renounce happiness; (iii) a man may choose to sacrifice his life at the call of duty, and so cut off any possibility of achieving further happiness; (iv) a man may organise his whole life in pursuit of a goal or in obedience to a rule which seems remote from happiness: for example the pursuit of truth, or obedience to the commands of an austere and all-demanding church or party.

These cases illustrate different ways in which putative counter-examples to the thesis that we all necessarily pursue only happiness might be advanced. The first three cases all concern someone who may well pursue happiness as an end, but it turns out not to be his only final end, since it is sacrificed for another end; the last case concerns someone for whom happiness apparently may not be an end at all. Again, the first case is itself ambiguous; it may concern an alternative goal (honour or passion), pursuit of which might structure much of life, or it may concern just one case in which the claims of honour or passion are preferred to those of happiness.

It might be said that the second and third cases, those in which duty is said to take precedence over happiness, are not cases of a competing *end* at all, but of a competing *rule*: a man who does something because it is his duty is not doing something in order to get something else. This distinction between an end and a rule is not however very substantial in this context. It is true that a man who does his duty does so *in* doing something specific, so doing his duty is not a caused result of his action. But if a man acts for the sake of duty, doing his duty is still the end of his action, in the sense that it is only because the action is seen as a duty that it is done; he could say, 'My sole purpose is to do my duty.' What can be said is that duty (on most views of it) is not an end the pursuit of which could relevantly govern *every* choice in one's life. The claims of duty in themselves, then, would present a possible *additional* final end, not an alternative single final end. The fourth case might be seen in terms of duty too. Alternatively, it may be seen in terms of an *ideal*, which is not espoused out of duty but which is not seen in terms of happiness either.

The obvious tactic, in trying to meet these alleged counter-examples to the necessity-of-the-pursuit-of-happiness thesis, is to try to show that they are all misdescribed, and that if they are redescribed appropriately they will support rather than oppose the thesis. Thus it might be said that all these cases, since they are all deliberate choices, are cases of a man structuring his life in accordance with rules or goals which he has purposely embraced. If so, then such a life, however bizarre it may seem to others, just *is* the kind of life which the man in question thinks will best please him: in other words, bring him happiness.

But this solution is not consistent with my earlier definition of happiness. For according to that definition a man is not happy if there is some important thing wrong with his life. So a man who renounces a brilliant career on which he had set his heart, because for example he thinks its demands on him will not be fair on his wife, cannot be described as happy, because his life lacks something on which he sets great store. Of course he may 'get over' the loss and find happiness in other things; but this need not happen and he need not expect it to. When making the choice he takes on a life which he expects to be deficient in an important way, and so he cannot be described as conforming to the principle that one should seek only happiness.

An objection might be raised here which is a consequence of another aspect of my account of what happiness is. I said earlier that readiness to hold on to one's situation is the chief sign of being pleased with it, or happy. Now it seems to follow that if a man makes a choice 'for duty's sake', as we say, and is ready to abide by the situation which is the result of his choice, this must *mean* that he is happy with that situation, since readiness to hold on to a situation is the chief sign of being pleased with it, or happy. The implication of this argument would be that it is logically impossible to sacrifice one's own happiness, except temporarily by mistake as the result of a miscalculation; anyone who makes a choice and is prepared to stick by it has by definition chosen happiness.

To counter this argument, and to clarify further my account of the nature of happiness, I will now make a distinction which has not been made hitherto: that between being *prepared* to stick to a certain situation or way of life (what I shall call acquiescence) and being *pleased* with it. Both alike are to be contrasted with changing or trying to change the situation, and so they can both be described, misleadingly, as wanting to hang on to a situation; but the kind of wanting is very different in the two cases. (We may call the kind of wanting which constitutes acquiescence 'being willing', the kind which constitutes being pleased 'desiring': thus to say that a man acquiesces in his situation is to say only that he is willing to hold on to it, not that he is desirous of doing so.)

My thesis then is that a person logically can, and sometimes does, deliberately choose to bring about a situation in which he will be acquiescent rather than pleased. I will illustrate this distinction in terms of the man who (as I should say) sacrifices his happiness for duty's sake. He does of course abide by his choice once made, but this acquiescence differs from being pleased in two ways: he is acting on a judgement, and he is acting against the grain. Let me say a little on each of these points.

The judgement in question is the judgement that the course he has adopted is indeed his duty; should he become convinced that he was mistaken in his judgement, he will, if he is rational, try to alter his course, since it is only because he sees it as his duty that he acquiesces in it. It may be said that what I have called being pleased with a situation depends on a judgement too, namely the judgement that the situation is pleasant. But this is not a judgement in the same sense, since error is not possible. A man can cease to be pleased with a situation which he previously liked. But if this happens he will not say that he was previously mistaken and has come to realise his error; he will say that his feelings have *changed*.

The second difference between acquiescence and being pleased is that the former is against the grain. This difference is difficult to bring out without invoking the very concept of being pleased which needs explaining. I said earlier that being pleased can be analysed in terms of what a man *does*. But it might seem that what he *does* is the same whether the case is one of being pleased or of acquiescence. This is true however only in broad terms; in detail there will be considerable differences. Thus the man who is pleased with his life will be resistant to suggestions that there is some reason to change it, whereas the man who has chosen his life on principle will look for ways of changing his life so as to accommodate his principle more amenably. The man who is happy does not seek distractions or escapes or ways to make the time pass, whereas the man of duty who is not happy will do these things. The man who is happy is at ease and relaxed with regard to his life, the unhappy man is subject to conflict and tension. The happy man finds that the various aspects of his life are enhanced by his happiness, whereas the unhappy man is hampered in his life by his unhappiness. And so on. Of course I am not denying that it is possible for some people in some cases to achieve *resignation*, the suppression of all rebellious thoughts and feelings. Such resignation may perhaps turn into happiness later on. But this is not to say that there is no difference from the start between the happy man and the man who chooses an unhappy life as a result of obedience to a principle.

Since it is possible to draw this distinction between being pleased with life and acquiescence in it, we can reject the claim that a man necessarily chooses the course which he thinks will lead to *happiness*. It may be that he necessarily chooses a course in which he thinks he will *acquiesce* once it is chosen. Indeed, to deny *this* necessity would be to say that a person can know, *before* he has chosen, that he will reverse his choice as soon as it is made – which would certainly be paradoxical. But a man can choose, knowing that what lies ahead of him may not rise above acquiescence.

These considerations, drawn from the duty situation, are sufficient in themselves to rebut the claim that people always choose the course they think leads to happiness. But it might be said that they do so more often than my list of counter-examples would suggest, on the grounds that everyone who acts for the sake of some *ideal*, rather than for duty's sake, finds in the ideal an attraction so overwhelming that any life in which it is realised, whatever else it lacks, is a life the idealist is pleased to live. This feature, it might be said, is what *defines* an ideal, as opposed to a duty; and so many non-duty cases, of the pursuit of honour or of passion, of truth or of a political Utopia, can be seen as the pursuit of happiness of an unusually narrow kind.

But even the realisation of an ideal will not provide a foolproof recipe for happiness. For even if we grant that ideals always attract rather than oblige, and even if we allow that an ideal may attract so much that a man may govern his life by it, it will not necessarily prevent his looking wistfully over his shoulder at things he has had to give up. Such a man is a long way from mere acquiescence, but he may know some measure of the conflicts which belong to the acquiescent man, and so fall short of the attainment of happiness. In any case, sometimes an ideal is seen, not as attractive or pleasant, but in ways which are like those associated with duty: as demanding or imperative, for example – or the devotee is described as 'in the grip of' or 'obsessed by' some idea, 'against his better judgement'. I conclude that those who pursue an ideal do not necessarily think they will achieve happiness by its realisation, any more than do those who do their duty in difficult circumstances.

These conclusions, however, though they are very significant for my account of happiness, would not of themselves rebut the claim that everyone ultimately seeks only happiness, *if* that is understood to mean 'happiness *or* the nearest to happiness that can be attained'. For it might be said that the people we have been discussing should be described not as those who sacrifice a happiness which they might have had, but as those who choose a prospect of lesser unhappiness rather than a prospect of greater unhappiness. For example, it might be said that a man who cares so much about duty could not possibly be happy in any case while living a life which depends on what he sees as defiance of it; what he necessarily does is to choose the life which he thinks will bring the nearest to happiness that he can get. (It is perhaps by a rather doubtful extension of this claim that the champions of the happiness thesis might try to accommodate the man who sacrifices his *life* out of a sense of duty, or indeed the man who commits suicide, from any motive. These people cannot be described as acting for the sake of *happiness*, but can perhaps, it will be argued, be described as acting to avoid the unhappiness which will be attendant on their staying alive.)

Now this thesis, that people do their duty, when they do, only because they think they will achieve the least unhappiness thereby, is open to two major objections. Firstly, it seems perfectly possible that a person may do what he thinks to be right while believing that he can if he wishes suppress his nagging conscience if he does the wrong thing more easily than the disappointment that will ensue if he does the right thing at great loss to himself. His belief may be *mistaken*, but that is not at issue. Secondly, a person may leave his conscience, easy or troubled, out of the reckoning altogether, and on that basis assume (perhaps wrongly, but again that is irrelevant) that he is choosing the path that will lead to more unhappiness than the other would have done, but still press on and do what he thinks to be right. Indeed, the view that people always act in order to achieve the least unhappiness makes it difficult to make sense of the anguish that sometimes accompanies deciding to do one's duty.

It might now be asked why it should be thought that everyone necessarily pursues only happiness as his ultimate end. Part of the answer, as we have seen, lies in the tendency to equate happiness with the several goals we seek for their own sakes. It thus becomes analytic that the only thing which we seek for its own sake is happiness; but this analytic truth is won at the cost, not only of substituting things for an attitude in the analysis of happiness, but of fragmenting it completely. If, on the other hand, it is realised that happiness consists in being pleased with things, not the things themselves, the source of the mistake must be different. I suspect that it arises as a result of the ambiguities in the notion of *wanting*. There *is* a sense of 'wanting' in which it is analytic that we choose to do something because it is what we want most to do. But it does not follow that we choose because we think that the result will be what we will want, in the *desiring* sense, to hang on to; and it is this latter wanting which is involved in happiness.

There is another possible source of the tendency to believe

that everyone pursues only happiness as his ultimate goal: the belief that this is the only rational policy and that human beings are rational creatures. But it is not clear that 'rational' is being used in the same sense in these two premises. I suggest that human beings are rational creatures in the sense that they often do things for *reasons* in terms of which they themselves see their actions and other human beings can understand why they act. In *this* sense of 'rational', acting for the sake of happiness is not the only rational policy, since it seems perfectly possible for someone to see himself as acting against his own happiness for duty's sake, or for the sake of some other idea, and for others to understand his so acting, at least in some measure.

It might of course be maintained that acting for the sake of happiness is the only rational policy in a *stronger* sense of 'rational': for example, that such a policy is to be *commended* in some way. I shall consider this view in chapter 4. But it cannot at the same time be maintained that human beings are rational in the sense that they always act in this commendable way. For if they were, the notion of commendation would be meaningless.

4 *Happiness as a Possible Final End*

There are three types of argument which purport to show that happiness is *not* a possible final end: (i) a logical argument, to the effect that happiness is not the kind of thing which can be pursued; (ii) a psychological argument, to the effect that pursuing happiness is self-defeating because to pursue it is to destroy its foundation; (iii) a practical argument, to the effect that the future is too unpredictable to make any long-term project worthwhile or even possible.

The logical argument has several sub-forms. According to one of these, happiness logically cannot be pursued for its own sake because it is always a by-product of getting other things, which *were* pursued for their own sakes. This is the version of an anti-psychological-hedonism argument, as applied to happiness, which I mentioned in the previous section; the idea is that if one tries to pursue other things as a means to happiness, one will necessarily fail, as one gets happiness only by pursuing things for their own sake and achieving them. As I said earlier,

I would reject this argument, because it mistakes the relationship between happiness (being pleased with one's life) and wanting. There is in fact no necessary connection between *having* wanted a certain situation and being pleased with it once one gets it. The connection is between being pleased and wanting to hang on to it now. It is true that wanting it now is equivalent to having 'really wanted' it before. It may also be true that 'really wanting' must involve some disposition which existed throughout. But it is clear that 'really wanting' is not the same as wanting in the sense which involves pursuing, so as far as this argument goes there is no logical reason why one should not pursue happiness.

A second type of logical argument challenges the appropriateness of talking of happiness as an end at all. In the case of most ends, the means are logically separable from them: thus if I play the piano to earn money, it makes sense for a fairy godmother to say, 'Forget about the playing; here is the money.' But this does not apply to happiness. If I marry in order to be happy it would not make sense for her to say 'Forget about the marriage, here is the happiness', since the happiness I sought (the argument goes) was by definition happiness in marriage. In the same way people argue that pleasure is not to be seen as an end to which its source is a means, since one logically cannot have the pleasure apart from its source, whereas means and ends are supposed to be connected only contingently.[11]

In answer to this argument it can be granted that happiness is necessarily always a reaction to one's situation, just as pleasure (of which happiness is after all a special kind) is necessarily a reaction to something which may be termed its source. It is also true that one necessarily cannot get happiness *in marriage* without being married, just as one necessarily cannot get the pleasure *of skiing* without skiing. But whether marriage brings happiness, or skiing pleasure, to a particular person remains an empirical matter; so a man is not for this reason logically debarred from seeking happiness as such *via* the achievement of some particular situation. Indeed, a person can want happiness in the abstract, without yet envisaging any particular situation from which it is to arise. Teenagers, asked what they plan to do in life, what their ambitions are and so on, are often quoted as replying, 'I don't have any plans – I don't know what I want to be – I just want to be happy.' (In the same way, a person can want *enjoyment* as such: 'I want to do something *enjoyable* this evening for a change.')

No doubt the relationship between pleasure or happiness and its source is not a very typical end–means relationship– for one thing means and end are here simultaneous, whereas in many cases the means precedes the end – but then there are very many different kinds of means–end relationship. And in the most important way the relation between pleasure or happiness and its source is exactly like that of end and means: if I do something because I think I will enjoy it, or adopt a way of life because I think it will bring happiness, and the expected pleasure or happiness does not ensue, I will regard my activity or my policy as *failures*, and will seek (other things being equal) to avoid the former in future and to reverse the latter.

It might still be claimed that there is no difference in practice between pursuing the attitude or reaction of happiness and pursuing any group of things for their own sakes. But this is not so. Firstly, things such as virtue or love can, as we saw, be pursued for their own sakes even when they are seen as *inimical* to the pursuer's happiness. Secondly, happiness is an attitude to one's life as a whole, so any one thing which can be described as done 'for the sake of happiness' must be sufficiently wide-ranging to affect one's life as a whole. Thus a person might say that he chose to emigrate, to get married, or to change his career 'because he thought he would be happier as a result'; but he could scarcely say this of a decision to go to France for his holidays or to learn Esperanto, unless he envisaged these things as affecting his whole life.

The third point which distinguishes the pursuit of happiness from the pursuit of specific things is that the former is largely carried on in ways which do not involve the pursuit of specific things at all. For example, the type of teenager I mentioned before might set about the pursuit of happiness by trying to find out what kind of temperament and aptitudes he has and what kind of life is likely to suit him. There are many psychological tests purporting to help in such enquiries. Or a person who realises he is *not* happy may undertake a review of his life in all its aspects and try to work out how he can improve it. Such an activity might be seen as a way of pursuing happiness, but it is not the pursuit of any specific thing. Again, a person may come to realise that in order to achieve all the various things he wants in life, and which he hopes can be integrated into a pleasing life, he needs to work out some kind of strategy in terms of the order of priorities, the temporal order in which goals are to be pursued, ways of combining them, and so on. This creating of a strategy is another 'second-order' activity which cannot be reduced to the pursuit of particular things. Again, a person may come to realise that one thing which he wants cannot be achieved without sacrificing everything else, or at all; and may set about trying to talk himself out of wanting it, or at least of setting so much store by it. This is not the pursuit of a *thing*, but an attempt to change one's feelings. Similarly he may see that he cannot basically alter an unpromising situation in which he finds himself, and so set about trying to change his attitudes, since he cannot change his circumstances.

These last points go some way towards quelling an uneasiness that people may still feel about the idea that happiness, a *reaction* to one's circumstances, can be wanted as distinct from wanting one's circumstances to be of a certain kind. It *does* seem possible to want to be at ease with or in tune with one's circumstances: to want something which might be achieved either by working on one's circumstances or on one's attitudes to them or both. One can certainly be weary of being 'at odds with' one's situation, without knowing even whether the situation or oneself should change, let alone having specific desires as to one's circumstances. Again, a person can sigh for his lost happiness while knowing that circumstances have not altered and that what has changed is his own attitude.

I conclude then that there is no logical impossibility in the pursuit of happiness, and turn to the second kind of argument: that the pursuit of happiness is *psychologically* impossible, because those who are always calculating how to achieve happiness destroy the spontaneous absorption in things from which happiness springs. This argument need not detain us for long, because it seems plausible only in an extreme case. Certainly a person who thinks *too much* of achieving happiness, who is for example always examining his attitude to his life to see what it is, may inhibit the unforced pleasure in aspects of his life which happiness requires. But it is surely plausible to maintain that an occasional review of one's situation and reordering of priorities makes one *more* likely to achieve happiness than living a completely unreviewed life. The trouble is that the psychological thesis, that concentrating too much on happiness interferes with spontaneous reactions to aspects of one's life, is apt to be confused with the version of the logical thesis which says that since happiness depends on getting specific things that you want it logically cannot itself be pursued. But as we saw this version of the logical argument is invalid.

Of course no amount of planning will *guarantee* happiness, as distinct from making it more likely, and here we come to the third kind of claim that the pursuit of happiness is impossible. Those who espouse this practical form of the argument can point to the uncertainty of achieving what one plans, uncertainty about one's own future reactions, and the possibility of disaster striking and destroying happiness. These arguments all presuppose that the stoic view, that happiness can be achieved in *any* circumstances, is mistaken. I would agree that happiness, in my sense of the term, cannot always be achieved; but I would see the points put forward by the practical pessimists as showing only that happiness cannot be guaranteed, not that it cannot be pursued. Nor does this kind of argument show even that it is pointless to pursue happiness, unless it be maintained that it is pointless doing anything unless one is sure of succeeding.

5 *Happiness as One of Everyone's Goals*

I have tried to show that, while happiness is not everyone's sole final goal, it is a possible final goal. The question which remains, then, is whether it is *a* final goal (perhaps one of several) for everybody.

At first sight it might seem that the answer is a fairly easy yes – surely, it might be said, everyone at some time or another does *something* for the sake of happiness, and this is all that is required. Now it may be true that everyone at some time or another does something for the sake of *pleasure* – indeed it would scarcely make sense to deny this. But to act for the sake of being pleased with one's *life* is a very different matter.

Some people clearly do this some of the time. There is a kind of person who imagines, in some detail, an ideal way of life for himself with which he believes he will be pleased – indeed, he imagines himself in the picture, *being* pleased – and who sets about realising this dream. Again, a man can want various (at first unconnected) things which he thinks will please him, and then set about working out how these wants can be jointly realised. Again, as we saw in the previous section, a person who decides that he is *not* happy may set about altering this, by altering either the situation or his attitude.

All these are cases of the pursuit of happiness, as distinct both from the pursuit of a thing as such and from the pursuit of pleasure in a specific thing. The pursuer's goal is to be pleased with his situation, not the situation as such. In many cases his pursuit takes the form of trying to attain concrete goals. But he would not pursue these goals unless he thought he would be pleased with the overall situation which they would constitute, just as a person who pursues something for the sake of pleasure would not pursue it if he thought pleasure would not attend the achievement of it. The person who pursues happiness may do a certain amount of imagining and experimenting to try to assure himself that what he is pursuing will in fact make him happy. Or he may simply assume that what makes others happy will make him so, or that if he wants some kind of life for the sake of happiness he will be pleased with it when he gets it. (I do not think it is *analytic* that people assume that they will be pleased with what they want for the sake of pleasure. There seem to be counter-examples: for example, a person can want to go to a party for the sake of enjoying it, while being doubtful about whether he will enjoy it.)

But if this is the pursuit of happiness, it seems quite easy to imagine that there are people who do not pursue happiness in this way. For example, there might be people who pursue several aims but make no attempt to see these as forming any kind of coherent 'life'; or people who are actually miserable but do nothing about it; or people whose whole life is taken up with some cause which leaves no room for the pursuit of happiness; or people who reject the thought of pursuing happiness because they think that happiness cannot be achieved by pursuing it. I say there 'might be' such people; I think there actually are, but this would be an empirical claim, and all I am concerned with is to suggest that these are comprehensible cases of people who do not pursue happiness at all.

It might now be said that at least everyone must *want* happiness. But this is not obviously true either. I am not primarily thinking of the point that it is not clear what wanting consists of where it does not involve trying to get. The doctrine that wanting involves trying to get is sound only if we add 'all other things being equal', and in the case of wanting happiness there are various reasons which would explain why a person might want happiness and not try to get it: for example, he might think that trying to get it is self-defeating; or that he is in such a bad position that he cannot possibly attain it; or that for some reason he does not deserve happiness. Rather I have in mind the possibility that some people do not think about happiness at all, and so *a fortiori* cannot be said to want it. A person might not (again, I would hold that some actually do not) consider the notion of being pleased with his life as a whole; perhaps because he is in general a rather unreflective person; or because he is too immersed in particular worries to look outside them; or because he has too weak a sense of self, being totally wrapped up in others' causes.

Nor is it even the case that a person who is positively unhappy must wish to get rid of his unhappiness. For a person can be unhappy without even realising he is unhappy, just as he can be happy without realising he is happy. No doubt such a person is aware of various dissatisfactions and miseries in different parts of his life; but he need not reach the point of totting them up, as it were, and saying to himself, 'I am distressed by my life as a whole.'

People will now insist that despite these remarks there must be a sense in which everyone *really* wants happiness. But it will be recalled that the phrase 'really wants' can have two meanings. It can be contrasted with 'pretends not to want'. But it cannot be maintained that a person who does not think of happiness, because he is too bound up in particular worries for example, is simply pretending to himself or others not to want it while in fact wanting it. The other meaning of 'really wanting' something was being pleased with it, wanting to hang on to it, when it is achieved. Can we say that everyone 'really wants' happiness in that sense?

The first reaction to this question is to wonder whether it

even makes sense: can one meaningfully be said to be pleased to be pleased with one's life, or do these two layers of being pleased collapse into one? There are certain phenomena which suggest that it *does* make sense, and that the answer to the question whether *everyone* who is happy is pleased to be happy is in fact no. I am thinking of the cases where a person is said to be *ashamed* of being happy: perhaps because he lives in the midst of a great deal of suffering on others' parts; or because he has recently been bereaved and thinks that his quick restoration to happiness shows him to be a man of shallow feelings; or because his life is so sordid and impoverished that he feels that a man of spirit should not be happy in such circumstances. If this shame is more than an agreeable twinge of self-criticism – if it leads its possessor to say 'I wish I weren't happy', as shame proper should logically do – then it might seem that we have a type of case where people are happy but are not pleased to be happy.

This is not however a really appropriate way to describe the situation, since worries about whether one is callous, or shallow, or lacking in self-respect are themselves relevant to one's happiness or lack of it. What we really have here is the difference between a partial and a total scope for happiness: the former comprising an attitude only to one's external situation, the latter comprising not only this but also an attitude to oneself, one's character and feelings. The man who was described as happy but not pleased to be happy would be better described as someone who is not entirely happy; he is happy about his circumstances, but precisely because of that he is unhappy about himself, and so unhappy overall, since being happy requires freedom from major distresses.

I would suggest, then, that everyone who is happy must logically be pleased to be happy, because it is impossible to say of anyone that he is not pleased to be happy without thereby entailing that from a more comprehensive point of view he is not happy. It is only in this sense that everyone wants to be happy.

2   Eudaemonia

1   *The Concept of* Eudaemonia

The kind of happiness which I have considered so far, and which I have maintained to be the most usual colloquial sense of the term 'happiness', is what may be termed *hedonistic* happiness: that is, it is to be defined in terms of pleasure, not in the sense of a surplus of pleasure over pain, but in the sense of being pleased with one's life. There is, however, another sense of the term which is now perhaps archaic, as far as colloquial usage is concerned: that signifying 'truly fortunate' or 'truly well-off' or 'possessed of true well-being'. The idea behind this notion is that he who is happy in this sense has what is *worth* desiring and worth having in life. I shall call this kind of happiness eudaemonistic happiness, or *eudaemonia* for short, and I would claim that my account of *eudaemonia* is, broadly speaking, an account of what Aristotle meant by the term in the *Nicomachean Ethnics*. The term *eudaemonia* is always translated simply as 'happiness' in English. But in view of the differences I am about to point out between Aristotle's concept and that conveyed by the term in its colloquial use, I would regard this translation as misleading; and when I use the terms 'happy' and 'happiness' without qualification, I shall always mean *hedonistic* happiness.

The main difference between *eudaemonia* and hedonistic happiness is that the former is attributed in terms of some kind of objective valuation, whereas the latter is attributed merely in terms of the kind of life the possessor in fact *wants* to hold on to. The latter attribution may be called a valuation too; at least, we can certainly say that the happy person *values* his way of life – and for present purposes I shall call this kind of valuation a subjective valuation. (It may of course be expressed in objective-seeming *language*: thus, a person can say 'It's a good life', meaning no more that 'I like it', 'I am happy'.) It is difficult to explain what I mean by 'objective' except by saying 'not subjective in the sense given above'. But I would hold that when someone speaks of something as *worth* wanting or *worth* having he is saying something objective, at least in this sense: that he would claim that what he says is true (or valid or sound) and that its truth is independent of his views on the matter. It would follow that attributions of *eudaemonia* logically can be subject to *error*, whether the man whose *eudaemonia* is in question makes the attribution or someone else. In other words, a man may *wrongly* say that his own life is *eudaemon* or worth having, whereas he cannot be wrong about a sincere claim that he is happy, as we said earlier.

This account of course presupposes that there is such a thing as objective valuation. There are those who would claim that no one does make a valuation which he sees as sound, valid or true, and that the difference which I have described in these terms is really only a difference between two kinds of *subjective* valuation: for example, between liking something and being prepared to commit oneself and others to it. But I find it difficult to believe that people never think of themselves as claiming some kind of validity for their valuations. Whether they are justified metaphysically in their claim – whether there are objective *values*, as well as objective *valuations* – is quite another matter.

It might be thought that what I am really talking about when I speak of objective valuation is valuation in terms of *reasons*, as opposed to subjective valuation, which is reasonless. For while it is true that typically a man can give reasons why he is happy in terms of a more detailed description of what his life is like, he cannot give reasons why the life thus described *pleases* him; in the end, he simply wants to hold on to it for its own sake, and any further explanation would have to be in terms other than reasons. But the giving of reasons is neither a necessary nor a sufficient criterion of what I have called objective valuation. It is not sufficient in that a prescriptivist account of valuation, while remaining subjective in my sense, draws a distinction between those valuations which rest on universalised reasons and those which do not. And it is not necessary, because one could imagine the possibility of someone's saying that he held a certain way of life to be worthwhile, or certain things to be worth having or getting, without being able to give any reason for his valuation. Indeed, it might be said that reasons for valuing things must come to an end somewhere, and that although various criteria have been employed for determining what kinds of thing are worth having (I shall consider some of them later in the chapter) there must still come a point at which one simply says: these are just the right criteria, it is right to value things in terms of these criteria and not others.

Before I leave the notion of objective valuation, I must remove two possible misconceptions. Firstly, what I have said about the objectivity of *eudaemonia* does not of itself imply that *eudaemonia* would consist of the same things for each person. On the contrary, it is possible to imagine a criterion for possessing *eudaemonia* which would give a different specification of it for each individual: for example, a criterion involving maximum deployment of individual talents. (Aristotle's own criterion, of course, was not individualistic in this way, appealing instead to a generalised conception of human nature.) Secondly, the objectivity of the concept of *eudaemonia* does not imply that there is *no* logical connection between *eudaemonia* and hedonistic happiness. It may for example emerge that any life which constitutes *eudaemonia* is also a life which brings hedonistic happiness, and even that what makes a man pleased with such a life is partly that it constitutes *eudaemonia*. The connections between *eudaemonia* and hedonistic happiness will be discussed in chapter 3. For the present I wish only to stress that the attribution of *eudaemonia* on the one hand and of hedonistic happiness on the other involves two different kinds of valuation: the latter rests only on the wishes of an individual with regard to his life, the former is essentially independent of these.

It will be noted that I spoke of a way of life as constituting *eudaemonia*, but as bringing hedonistic happiness. In other words, I am construing *eudaemonia* and hedonistic happiness as belonging to different categories: *eudaemonia* is constituted by a way of life, whereas hedonistic happiness is a reaction to a way of life. I have maintained this difference because it reflects the difference I sense between the discussion in Aristotle, about what *eudaemonia* consists in, and everyday modern discussions about what brings happiness or makes people happy. One

could of course mark off a concept in the same category as
(indeed, a particular case of) hedonistic happiness to relate to
eudaemonia: namely respectable hedonistic happiness, or being
pleased with a way of life which constitutes *eudaemonia*. There
would be two kinds of respectable hedonistic happiness, according to whether or not the being pleased depended on the
recognition that the way of life was a case of *eudaemonia*. I shall
discuss in chapter 3 the question whether a man who possesses
eudaemonia always possesses this respectable hedonistic happiness, and if so of which kind. I shall also consider whether the
possession of *eudaemonia entails* the possession of hedonistic
happiness, in the sense that we would not say that a man has
eudaemonia unless he is hedonistically happy.

I shall now try to grasp the nettle of the phrase 'fit to be
wanted' in the definition of *eudaemonia*, a phrase which by
implication I equated to 'worth having in life'. The sense of 'fit'
or 'worth' here needs some discussion. It seems that something
of a dilemma arises. Either we construe 'fit to be wanted' and its
equivalents in prudential terms, in which case it seems that
eudaemonia collapses into hedonistic happiness after all and loses
its objective standards; or we construe them in moral or
quasi-moral terms, in which case *eudaemonia* loses any necessary
connection with what its possessor actually wants and so any
claim to be a kind of *happiness*, as we normally understand the
term. Colloquially, the idea of something as 'worth *having*'
tends to suggest appeal to a prudential range of considerations,
whereas the ideas of activities as 'worth *doing*' and of a worthwhile *life* (and perhaps of the kind of person it is worth *being*, or
being like) suggest a quasi-moral approach. But it should
always be noted that in this kind of context the distinctions
between being, doing and having are not always sharp. Thus
one can speak of the worthwhileness of *being* an artist, or of
having the life of an artist, or of spending one's time *doing* art.
Again, one can speak either of courage as a quality worth
having, or of the courageous man as the kind of man it is worth
being.

It might be said that a difference can after all be made
between the concepts of hedonistic happiness and a prudential
version of *eudaemonia*: hedonistic happiness is what any individual experiences who is in fact pleased with his life, whereas
eudaemonia is the life with which any individual *would* be most

highly pleased if he were to experience it – the life which offers the greatest possible degree of hedonistic happiness. Such a concept would allow for objectivity, in the sense that applications of it would be verified, not by asking an individual about his own life, but by generalisàtions about human wishes and human nature. Thus even if a man said truly that he was happy, he might still be wrong about whether his life constituted *eudaemonia*, the greatest happiness of which he was capable. In this view, *eudaemonia* would be worth having in that it brought maximum happiness, and activities which contribute to *eudaemonia* would be worth doing in that they contributed to that happiness.

To many people, this account of *eudaemonia* would be quite sufficient. As far as they are concerned, to speak of a way of life as worth living would be simply to say that its practitioners are supremely *happy*, and to speak of an activity, such as scholarship or writing poetry, as worth doing would mean simply that those who practise it gain a particular and unique pleasure from it. Even Plato and Aristotle, when discussing what kind of life constitutes *eudaemonia*, seem to be thinking partly along these lines.[1] But such an account misses out the idea that people are *right* to like certain things better than others, and makes all valuation contingent on empirical facts about human nature.

It might still be maintained that all we need, and all we can have in the last analysis, is a valuation based on the *actual* inclinations of human beings. Such a view remains plausible if one thinks of human nature as a fixed quantity. But the difficulty of sustaining this position emerges if it is pointed out that human nature can be tampered with – in theory, and increasingly in practice; say, by drugs. Suppose it were possible to administer a drug, like Aldous Huxley's *soma*,[2] which makes people gain as much satisfaction from infantile games as they now more precariously do from the activities traditionally thought of as worthwhile: those who give a merely prudential account of *eudaemonia* have to say that the way to achieve a worthwhile life is to take *soma* and spend your days making mud pies. They are cut off from the possibility of saying, as most people would want to say, that the life of the scholar or artist is more worthwhile, even if less happy, than the life of the mud pie maker.

Nor can they escape by saying that a worthwhile life is the life

which makes *normal* human beings happiest. For one thing, the
question would arise why it should be worthwhile to lead the
life of a normal human being rather than, say, a drugged one – a
question which cannot be answered if 'worthwhile' means only
'productive of more happiness'. For another thing, the ground
for assessment of a human being as 'normal' will not necessarily
be clear. We can doubtless say of an extreme case, where a
person's whole nature is altered by drugs, that he is not to be
counted as a normal human being. But it may well be that
different kinds of upbringing affect the extent to which a person
is made happy by this or that thing: for example, the extent to
which he needs close personal relationships for happiness. If
this is so, how are we going to decide whether the person who is
more self-sufficient or the person who is more dependent counts
as normal?

I suggest, then, that it is difficult consistently to maintain the
position that the only ultimate valuation to be put on activities
is in terms of the degree of happiness they produce, and I
address myself henceforward to those who agree with me that
we sometimes need to be able to say that activities are worthwhile or that things are worth having in a sense which is to be
distinguished from that which refers to maximum happiness.

Two questions immediately arise: firstly, in what way does
eudaemonia relate to happiness of the hedonistic kind? And
secondly, in what way does talk about *eudaemonia* differ from
talk about morality? Both these questions deserve extended
discussion. The first question I shall consider in chapter 3. The
second question I shall discuss in chapter 4, considering how
far *eudaemonia* is a name for a set of duties or can plausibly be
said to give rise to duties, whether these duties would be to
ourselves, to others or to the worthwhile ingredients of
eudaemonia themselves, and whether it would be better to talk of
ideals, rather than duties, in this sphere.

2   Eudaemonia *as Good in Itself*

So far, I have spoken of *eudaemonia* using the terminology of
what is *fit* to be wanted, *worth* wanting, and so on. I might
equally well have said that '*eudaemonia*' means 'a way of life
which is *good in itself*'. I cannot go into all the many uses of the

word 'good' here and their various connections with the concepts of wanting and choice. In many of these uses (some philosophers would say all)[3] a thing is explicitly or implicitly said to be a good such-and-such: in other words, it is judged with reference to a class to which it belongs. But I would maintain that something can also be said to be just 'good', or 'a good thing'. These expressions can be used to convey either what I called a *subjective* valuation (as when someone getting into a hot bath after a tiring day says 'This is good' meaning 'This is nice, I like this'), or an *objective* valuation, as when people say knowledge is good or a good, meaning that it is worth wanting or pursuing. The phrase 'in itself', like the adverb 'intrinsically', is often in philosophical parlance attached to the word 'good' to make clear that this objective valuation is in question, and so using this terminology *eudaemonia* can be said to be good in itself.

The phrase 'good in itself', again like 'intrinsically good', can also mean 'good as an *end*', as distinct from 'good as a means'. As has often been said, the same thing can be both. But if a thing is good only as a means, it is wanted, or fit to be wanted, only because it is a means to something else; whereas if something is good as an end it is wanted or fit to be wanted for its own sake. (The two formulae, 'wanted/fit to be wanted', refer to things said to be subjectively good and objectively good respectively; the subjective–objective distinction cuts right across the means–end one.) Thus one might say that exercise is good (wanted or worth wanting) only as a means to health, whereas health is good both as a means (because it enables its possessor to do things he could not do without it, for example) and as an end (it is wanted, or worth wanting, for its own sake).

I shall use the term '*eudaemonia*' to refer to a life which is good in itself, not only in the earlier sense of 'good by objective valuation', but also in this sense of 'good as an end': in other words, for a life which is worth having for its own sake. If, for example, the life of a medical missionary is good only because of its results (health and happiness brought to others) and the life of the artist is good, worth living, independent of results (fame, money, or whatever they may be) then the life of the artist is a candidate for *eudaemonia* and the life of the missionary is not.

There are, however, many difficulties with the idea of

eudaemonia as a life good as an end. Firstly, the distinction between the goodness of means and of ends is difficult to apply to whole ways of life, however natural it may be in other spheres; for a way of life is not as *homogeneous* as phrases like 'the life of the artist' suggest. The artist must now and again do some merely useful things (like washing the dishes) and the missionary may be a Schweitzer and spend his spare time in artistic pursuits. The distinction between the useful and the good in itself seems rather to be between activities, and perhaps other things as well.

We can however rescue the distinction between useful lives and lives good as ends if we see washing the dishes, playing the organ and so on as *ingredients* in a way of life; washing the dishes and administering the quinine might be merely useful ingredients, whereas painting pictures and playing the organ might be good in themselves. A way of life could then be said to constitute *eudaemonia* if the ingredients, good in themselves, predominate in it – the more they do so, the greater the degree of *eudaemonia*, so that if the artist has the washing-up done for him his life is more truly fortunate than if he has to do it himself. *Eudaemonia* is thus good on the whole rather than good through and through, to employ Ross's distinction.[4]

I should like to digress here to consider into what logical categories these things good in themselves must fall. The answer to this question is given by considering that these things good in themselves can form part of a way or style of life, and can be wanted and in some cases sought for their own sakes. I think that these considerations rule out objects, as such. This can be seen by considering possible counter-examples. Thus it might be said that works of art, such as pictures, are objects which might be said to be good in themselves. But a picture as such cannot be said to be part of someone's life; what might be part of someone's life is owning pictures, painting pictures, looking at pictures, thinking about pictures, and so on. Again, a picture cannot strictly speaking be wanted, as such; when a man says 'I want a picture', what is wanted is the owning of a picture. Moreover, if the picture is supposed to be wanted for its own sake, and not as, say, a hedge against inflation, then even 'owning a picture' is not really a sufficiently intelligible account; we should want to know what 'owning a picture' really amounted to in this man's life, and the answer would probably be in terms of his *contemplating* the picture.[5]

People (or rather, in this context, 'persons') are also sometimes spoken of as valuable in themselves or as ends in themselves (though not, I think, as *good* in themselves, which is significant). Now a man logically cannot aim at or want people, except by an elliptical way of speaking.[6] He can, however, aim at having various kinds of relationships with people, and this is the equivalent to aiming at having a picture to *enjoy* in some way.

Of course, the claim that people are valuable or worthwhile in themselves is not usually to be construed in this way, as a recommendation that *relationships* with people are worthwhile in themselves (though sometimes it is, as when someone says, 'People are worthwhile too', to an over-reclusive scientist or artist). More normally it is a way of making the claim that human life is sacred, or that other people's ends should be respected, or that what may be called 'personhood' – those characteristics which make a human being a person – should be fostered. None of these claims recommends any specific aim for us to pursue. The last of them yields instead a possible *criterion* in terms of which candidates for things good in themselves can be judged; it will be considered later in the chapter. The other two claims are really claims about the moral rules in accordance with which we should pursue our own aims and foster those of others – though, as we saw in chapter 1, 'doing one's duty' in general can be an aim in life.

I would suggest, then, that possible ingredients in a life to be pursued for its own sake cannot logically consist of objects, since an object is not as such part of a life. Moreover, mere possession of an object raises the question 'What does he want it for?', and so leads on to the idea of *enjoyment* of the object, in some sense of the word 'enjoy'. More broadly, one might say that activities, rather than objects, are appropriate candidates to be good in themselves.

In using the term 'activities' here, I am not necessarily committing myself to the Aristotelian distinction between *energeiai* (often translated 'activities') and *kineseis* (often translated 'processes').[7] Aristotle held that 'processes' such as painting a picture, which bring about a certain result by stages, are valued if at all only as means to a result, whereas 'activities' such as contemplation, which are 'complete' at any given point in time, can be valued for their own sakes. But there are two things wrong with this view. Firstly, it embodies a confusion between an activity's being directed towards or structured in terms of an end, and its being performed *for the sake of* that end.[8] If I paint a picture there is a sense in which what I do is directed towards producing an end-product, finished when it is finished, and so on. But it does not follow that I always paint a picture solely for the sake of having the end-product; I might tear up the picture as quite hopeless but still think the afternoon spent painting it was well spent. Secondly, the alleged distinction is at best between two ways of looking at what goes on, rather than between two different sorts of things which go on; the same happening can be viewed either as going for a walk (activity) or as journeying from South Tawton to South Zeal (process).

Perhaps these two objections are really two ways of putting the same objection. If so, it might be reasonable to adopt a modified version of Aristotle's thesis allowing for the objections, and say that activities which are directed towards some goal can be viewed as good in themselves only if they can be *seen as* having point in themselves apart from the realisation of the goal.

Aristotle thought also that *eudaemonia* must consist in activities rather than states; on this point he says that it is virtuous activity, rather than virtue, which is a possible candidate for *eudaemonia*.[9] It is not clear why he should wish to maintain this. In the case of virtue, indeed, the distinction is not of great importance, since a virtue is among other things a disposition to act in certain ways. But there are other cases, such as the possession of knowledge and of physical and mental health, where the connection with relevant activity is much weaker, and yet it seems intelligible to speak of seeking to possess knowledge for its own sake. One might indeed see some virtues (not in the Aristotelian canon) as more like species of knowledge than dispositions to action: humility, for example. It is true that to seek to be in certain states for their own sakes is to see *eudaemonia* in terms of being a certain kind of person, rather than leading a certain kind of life. But there seems no reason why a man's *eudaemonia* should not consist, or partly consist, in what he *is*.

Aristotle might also seem in stressing activities to be excluding *experiences*, and this is even less plausible, at least if we consider how inseparably bound up activity and experience are in some of the kinds of thing normally considered to be goods in themselves. For example, the contemplation of beauty surely involves both a deliberate paying of attention and studying and an emotional reaction. Again, the pursuit of personal relationships clearly involves certain activities and certain emotions. Again, even on Aristotle's own admission, virtue is manifested not only in actions but also in feelings. Nor does it seem possible to separate activity from experience in these cases, even in theory. To study a work of art or a landscape in nature without any emotional experience is not recognisable as the contemplation of beauty at all; to give alms to a beggar without sympathising with his woes is not the practice of the virtue of charity, and so on. Of course, Aristotle's contemplation of eternal truths may be possible without *emotion*; though even there one would be tempted to say that there must be experience bound up with activity, in that the contemplator is conscious of his activity. Certainly there seems no *a priori* reason to exclude experiences from the possible ingredients of *eudaemonia*.

I return now to my discussion of *eudaemonia* as good in itself. I said earlier that if the missionary's life is good only because of its results and the artist's is good independent of results, then the artist's life is a candidate for *eudaemonia* and the missionary's is not. But many people would find this claim difficult to reconcile with the idea that *eudaemonia* is the valuable or worthwhile life, in that they will feel inclined to object that the medical missionary's life is extremely valuable and worthwhile precisely *because* it is useful – and indeed that it is *more* valuable than the artist's for this reason.

Now I do not wish to deny that the medical missionary's life is very valuable, and that we might reasonably say, 'Better to be a good doctor than a poor artist', or even, 'Better to be a doctor than an artist' *tout court*. But this is quite consistent with the view that the doctor's life is good only as a means, only because of the health and happiness it produces in the world; in other words, that its value is *derivative* from the values of other things.

A further difficulty is that we are reluctant to say that

something like medicine is valuable *only* as a means. This reluctance can be brought out by considering what our reactions would be if it could be brought about that no one was ever ill or injured, so that there was no longer any point in the practice of medicine. I suggest that there would be aspects of medicine which we would be sorry to lose, and which must therefore have more than utilitarian value: the devotion and compassion of some doctors and nurses, the *cameraderie* which builds up between various medical workers, the exercise of skill and knowledge, and perhaps, for the religious, the service to God given through medicine by religious doctors and nurses.

The answer to this difficulty is to distinguish between the utilitarian activity, medicine as such, which is merely the activity of trying to bring about a certain valued result, and the other aspects or concomitants which, while often associated with medicine, can equally well be found in other spheres. It is the latter which justify the imputations of intrinsic value to medicine. Thus, for example, exercises of compassion and dutifulness may be good in themselves, and if this is so, then in so far as a particular doctor or nurse is acting dutifully or compassionately on a particular occasion his or her activity, *seen under that description*, is good in itself. If we see medicine as an empirical whole, including, as it in practice does, elements which can be termed good in themselves, then we will be inclined to say that it is to some extent good in itself. But if we define medicine, in Platonic style, as 'the art of producing health' then it is valuable merely as a means.

It should be noted that nothing I have said about medicine would imply that people should choose to become artists rather than doctors, or should encourage others to choose in this way. This might seem to follow if it is assumed that something which is valuable as an end must be more valuable than something which is valuable as a means. But this assumption is not obviously correct, if what the means brings about is an even larger quantity of the valuable end: in other words, if one doctor can save the lives of several artists. Similarly, even if one were to argue, in ideal utilitarian fashion, that our only duty was to maximise the good in itself, it might still be the case that for the majority this duty entailed, not living such a life themselves, but sustaining the fabric of society without which no such lives are possible. This view would, however, accord a very high status, in duty terms, to the good in itself; more plausible views would be, either that the promotion of this good is one *prima facie* duty among others, or that it is a moral ideal going beyond duty. Neither of these views (which I shall discuss further in chapter 4) would entail that people should become artists rather than doctors.

Before I leave this discussion of useful lives and lives good in themselves, I should like to point out the implications of my observation that medicine can be viewed as good in itself in so far as various activities involved in it can be seen under other descriptions: as exercises of the scientific intellect, as demonstrations of personal relationships in a working partnership, and so on. It seems to me that a great many ostensibly useful activities can have this kind of extra dimension. For example, cookery can be an aesthetic activity, washing up can be an act of friendship; any activity can be a religious activity: 'A servant with this clause Makes drudgery divine; Who sweeps a room as for Thy laws Makes that and the action fine.'[10] Whether or not an activity has this non-utilitarian resonance will depend sometimes on its motive, sometimes on the way it is regarded, sometimes on its conformity to standards other than the merely utilitarian ones. The consequence of this point is that it is possible to view many kinds of life, not merely the lives of leisure marked out by Aristotle, as exhibiting some degree of *eudaemonia*; and phrases like 'scientific activity', 'artistic activity' and so on, though they will usually refer primarily to 'pure' cases such as the professional artist painting a picture or the research biochemist looking down his microscope, will carry a secondary reference to these cases of doing a worthwhile activity *in* doing a useful one.[11]

3 *The Good in Itself and the Good for Man*

I shall now consider whether this concept of the life good in itself, which I have been developing, is the same as 'the good for man', of which one often hears. But this question has many different senses, according to what meaning is to be attached to the phrase 'good for man'. Certainly what is good in itself, as I have defined it, is not good for man in the sense that its

goodness depends on man's judgements or feelings, as in the
sense of 'for' employed by those who speak of propositions as
true for one person and not another. It *is* the good for man in that
the things which possess this goodness in itself are all states or
activities of *human beings*. (In so far as the good in itself is
thought of as necessarily *pursuable*, or at least *wantable*, I think
that must be so – though there might be senses of 'good in itself',
perhaps equivalent to 'to be worshipped or venerated', of which
this did not hold.)

The good in itself is not, however, the good for man in a third
sense: the sense of 'goodness in a man', that in virtue of the
possession of which a man is called a good man. The phrase 'a
good man' is in English reserved for the *morally* good man, and
whereas moral goodness has a special place in *eudaemonia*,
which I shall endeavour to locate in the next section, the two
ideas of the life good in itself and of moral goodness are quite
distinct. One might however be able to say that the man who
has *eudaemonia* provides a good *specimen* of human living at its
richest, employing a kind of biological metaphor; or alternatively that he is good *at* human living, in Aristotelian style.
Aristotle did apparently think that a man who possessed
eudaemonia must be called a good man in virtue of this.[12] But it is
clear that his idea of the good man in this context is something
like 'the man who is good at human living', by analogy with the
man who is good at some specific activity.

The good in itself is not, fourthly, the good for man in the
sense of being what man does in the end seek, his sole ultimate
purpose. I shall argue in chapter 3 that not everyone has a
conception of the good in itself, quite apart from making it his
final aim. Aristotle may still be right in saying that everyone
ultimately seeks the good as he sees it, but only if 'the good' can
cover both what the seeker thinks will be pleasant and what he
thinks is good objectively.

The question whether the good in itself is the good for man in
the sense of being what he *ought* to pursue or make his goal in life
I leave to chapter 4. It might be said that if something is good in
the objective sense of 'good', namely '*fit* to want', '*fit* to pursue',
and so on, it must follow that a man ought to pursue it. But
there are, as I have already said, various possibilities here, such
as that the good in itself involves ideals rather than duties.

The final sense of 'good for man', and the most important, is 'what is profitable to man, in his interests, conducive to his welfare'. Is the good in itself good for man in this sense? The trouble is that all these phrases are fatally *ambiguous*, at least if the tenor of my argument so far is sound. They might mean either 'what will in the end minister to man's desires, bring him happiness', or 'what will bring him nearer to the best he can be'. I have argued that the latter can be given a sense independent of the former, in the sense that a man can be said to live a life of high value where the value is not to be *reduced* to propositions about happiness or maximum happiness. If it be maintained that ideas of profit, interest and welfare cannot really be divorced from happiness, I should reply that one can quite easily imagine cases where they seem to diverge. Consider a very primitive tribe who seem blissfully happy in their way of life. Debate can meaningfully take place on whether they ought to be introduced to civilisation, whether for example we 'owe it to them' to give them opportunities to develop their minds, even if it is *agreed* that they will probably be happier if left alone and even if there is no one but themselves who will in any sense benefit.

The answer to the question whether the good in itself is in man's interest, then, depends on which sense of 'interest' (or 'profit', 'welfare', 'benefit') is at stake. If the question is whether *eudaemonia* makes a man happier, this is the topic discussed at length in chapter 3; I conclude there that whereas *eudaemonia* must by definition include happiness, it is not necessarily the only way to happiness. If the question is whether possession of the life good in itself is conducive to man's being the best he can be, I would say that this must be true by definition.

It might be objected that something cannot be both good in itself and good for man in this sense: if it is good in itself it is to be valued for its own sake, whereas if it is good for man it is to be valued for men's sakes. But if 'for its own sake' means 'as an end', this is not a true antithesis, as 'valuing for men's sakes' cannot mean 'valuing as a means to the end of men'. On the other hand, there *is* a possible conflict between seeing things as good in themselves as an ultimate valuation, and seeing them as good in themselves by virtue of some criterion of 'man's

distinctive endowment' or the like. In the latter case the
ingredients of *eudaemonia*, though still good as ends rather than
as means, would not be good in themselves in the special sense
that no·linking value could be discovered. Later in this chapter
I shall argue that giving a reason linking our judgements of the
goods in themselves is more persuasive than leaving them in an
unconnected bundle, and I shall discuss the criterion of the
distinctive human endowment.

There is another way in which, it might be said, the ideas of
the good in itself and the good for man may conflict; this
emerges if the good for man is construed as the welfare of
individuals, to which each has an *individual* claim, whether it be
welfare in the happiness or the *eudaemonia* sense. For the good in
itself, although necessarily realised in the lives of individuals,
can be pursued with no concern that *each* individual has any
right or claim. For example, the view that scholarship is good in
itself, regardless of who does it, might recommend a policy of
concentrating on the few who can do it most excellently;
whereas the view that each person's life ought to contain this
good as far as possible would favour a different policy. I shall
consider this problem in chapter 4. For the present, I shall
simply note that my speaking of something as good in itself is
not to be taken as a denial of the possibility of speaking of the
individual's rights to what is said to be good in itself.

4   *Morality as an Ingredient in* Eudaemonia

I have so far depicted *eudaemonia* as consisting of various
different ingredients held to be good in themselves, and I have
mentioned the practice of virtue, the doing of duty and so on, as
one among other possible ingredients of *eudaemonia*. But it might
be felt that the practice of morality must surely be *the* thing
which is good in itself, and the morally good life *the* life which is
worth living for its own sake. If something is worth wanting for
its own sake, then surely this is just another way of saying it is
one's moral duty; and if something is worth having, in some
non-prudential sense, then that surely means simply that one
morally ought to try to get it.

Two different theses must be disentangled here. The first
thesis does not in fact challenge the suggestions I have hinted

at, and will develop in the next section, about the multiform *content* of *eudaemonia*. It is concerned rather with the *concept* of *eudaemonia*, the *meaning* of saying that a thing is good in itself. It may be expressed in the proposition that statements about what is good in itself are to be analysed in terms of duties or obligations to bring about, to pursue, to foster, the thing in question. This thesis does not as a rule make the duty and the good thing identical. If what is alleged to be good is an activity, then it is true that *one* duty involved will be simply to perform it; but there might be other duties entailed even where the good *is* an activity (for example, to make opportunities to act, to learn how to act, to acquire the materials necessary, and so on). And some good things may not be activities at all, so that there can be no question in those cases of an identity between the doing of one's duty and the ingredient of *eudaemonia* in question. This thesis, that 'good in itself' can be translated in terms of duty, is to be discussed in chapter 4, as I have already said.

The second thesis is a thesis about the *content* rather than the concept of *eudaemonia*. According to the second thesis, *eudaemonia* has only one ingredient, morality itself: in other words, morality is the only thing which can be said to be good in itself, the latter notion being left undefined. I wish to try to dispose of the second thesis at this stage, since if it were valid it would cast doubt on my later procedure in this chapter, which assumes a list of several possible goods in themselves. (Note that the first thesis does not *entail* the second. We can say '"Good in itself" is translatable in terms of duty' without being committed to saying that morality is the only thing which we have this kind of duty to foster.)

Now 'morality' is a vague term which in this context might refer either to doing one's duty or to being virtuous, moral rightness or moral goodness. I shall start by considering the thesis that doing one's duty is the only thing good in itself. One possible objection to this view would be the claim that doing one's duty, so far from being good in *itself*, is good only as a means to other desirable things. The whole point of morality, it might be argued, is to bring about something else, harmony between conflicting interests, stability in society or whatever, and the reason why certain actions are right is that they do this.

This version of the doctrine that morality is good only as a means is crudely utilitarian, seeing good consequences as all of one kind and always to be maximised. But the claim that morality is good only as a means can also be made more subtly. There is plausibility in saying that a right action must be right because it brings about some benefit, of different kinds in different cases. For example, telling the truth is right because people acquire true beliefs thereby, keeping promises is right because people thereby gain benefits and services which they can rely on, sticking to one's post is right because only so can comrades' lives be defended, and so on. If doing one's duty is thus to be valued only as a means, it cannot be the only thing good in itself since it is not good in itself at all.

The champions of the thesis will object that doing one's duty has, by definition, a supreme *claim* on people, in the sense that if a person has a choice between two actions one of which is his moral duty, then there is no room for debate as to what he ought to do. Surely this means that doing one's duty is after all of supreme value?

In reply I would concede that moral duty is indeed supreme, in this sense, among actions, but point out that the proposition is quite consistent with the thesis that doing one's duty is valuable only as a means. For to say that the morally demanded action is the one which must be done is not to say that it is good as an *end*, only that it takes precedence over the alternative *actions*. This might be precisely *because* of the good consequences it brings about.

It might still be objected that duty necessarily takes precedence even over alternative actions which are themselves of a type which might be thought to be good in itself. For example, a man can have a duty to go and visit a sick relative in hospital even when he could spend the afternoon painting a picture instead. Surely, it might be argued, this means that doing one's duty is supremely good, since it is by definition better than other alleged goods in themselves?

But, as before, one might say that whereas to do one's duty must be in some sense better than the alternatives, even where these are good in themselves, it need not be good as an *end*. For the reason why a particular action is a duty might be that in the long run doing that kind of thing produces more goods in themselves than undertaking the worthwhile activities directly. In any case, we should look again at the proposition that duty takes precedence over goods in themselves. Either it means that duty is always what one ought to do, which is merely trivial, or it means that goods in themselves, as such, generate no duties. This latter proposition is really a denial of the *other* thesis, mentioned at the beginning of the section, that 'good in itself' is translatable in terms of duty. But, as we saw earlier, to deny this latter thesis is not to affirm that there is nothing other than doing one's duty which is good in itself.

It might be said that my treatment of duty is too *utilitarian* even in a broad sense of that term. Duty is important, not because it brings about certain results, but because allegiance to the moral law for its own sake is important. But this seems to be a thesis about dutifulness or conscientiousness, a quality of character or of the agent's will. It therefore belongs to the other aspect of morality, to which I now turn.

The other version of the thesis that morality is the only thing good in itself is in terms, not of doing duty as such, but of moral *goodness*: the possession of moral virtues, or in Kantian terminology the exercise of the dutiful will. We can agree that the exercise of moral virtues is often thought to be *a* good in itself, if we recall the discussion of whether the life of a doctor is good in itself; I said there that if the need for medicine were done away with, there might reasonably be regret at the loss of the exercise of compassion, devotion to duty, and so on, often involved. Similar points are often in fact made about the loss of scope for courage and self-sacrifice which would ensue if there were no wars – a point which, it should be noted, does not commit its maker to being in favour of war overall. In general, it seems that whereas the virtues are made necessary by deficiencies in man and his surroundings, they have a value which does not derive wholly from their usefulness in dealing with such deficiencies. We shall see in the next section how far various possible criteria for the ingredients of *eudaemonia* would explain this valuation.

But to maintain that moral virtue *is* good in itself is not to show that it is the *only* such good, that the only content for *eudaemonia* is simply moral virtue. This stronger thesis, however, is the one under discussion. Since it was maintained by Kant, in the form that the exercise of the dutiful will is the only thing good in itself,[13] I shall call it the Kantian thesis for ease of reference.

The Kantian thesis cannot be interpreted as meaning that

the exercise of the dutiful will (or of virtue) should be our sole
final end and that everything else should be done with a view to
that. For although (as we saw in chapter 1) there is a sense in
which being virtuous can be a final aim, dutifulness and virtue
leave room for, and indeed presuppose that we have, other aims
in life. Thus to say to someone, 'Be dutiful', or 'Be virtuous', is
not informative about what he should do in life in the way that
'Be a musician' is, since one can be or fail to be dutiful or
virtuous in pursuing many different goals in life. Indeed, it is
not altogether clear that one can pursue dutifulness (the
motive) at all.

Instead, one must construe the Kantian thesis as saying that
it does not matter, from the point of view of ultimate value,
what a person does in life so long as he is dutiful: in other words,
a good man, whatever his circumstances, possesses *eudaemonia*,
since he has the only thing which is really worth having. Even if
he is without friends or any opportunity for a cultivated life, his
life is as worthwhile as that of the man who has everything
normally thought of as worthwhile.

There are many reasons why someone might hold this thesis.
Firstly, he might think that the good man's life is in *practice*
complete in itself, because as well as moral virtue it must
contain other good things which are necessary for its exercise:
for example, friends to be the recipients of generosity.[14] But this
argument rests on a mistake about the nature of virtue as a
unified concept. The man on a desert island can perhaps not
practise *generosity*, but he can exercise virtue in general, if this
means exercising those moral qualities which are called for in
that situation. No one who retains the use of human faculties
can logically be in a situation where the exercise of virtue is
denied him.

The second and third arguments for virtue as the only
intrinsic good acknowledge this point and rest upon it. The
second argument starts from the idea that virtue is the only
utterly *safe* possession, the only thing which cannot be taken
away. It is then argued that virtue must be the only true good,
since a man's good fortune cannot consist or partly consist in
things which he may lose at any moment. The third argument
starts from the idea that virtue is the only possession which
everyone can have, whatever his circumstances and capacities;

and goes on to suggest that since 'the good for man' must be something available to everyone, it must consist in virtue.

Both these arguments tend to seem persuasive to anyone who is reluctant to allow that some people, through no fault of their own, cannot achieve *eudaemonia* and that others, having had it, lose it. But even if one granted the democratising premise, that *eudaemonia* must be an inalienable possession and possible for all, it would not follow that virtue is the only thing good in itself, the sole possible constituent of *eudaemonia*. What would follow would be the weaker view, to be discussed at the end of the section, that virtue is of such value that possession of it *can* constitute *eudaemonia* by itself.

The fourth argument lays stress on the *admiration* we feel for the man who preserves his virtue in the midst of the most difficult and uncongenial situations. He is surely to be congratulated and felicitated (the argument goes) and if so presumably he has achieved true good fortune, the life really worth having. This argument, however, confuses two reasons for admiration. We can indeed admire the achievement of the man who 'rises above' impossible circumstances, as well as that of the man who achieves *eudaemonia*, who shows what human life at its best can be like. But it does not follow that it is the man who rises above impossible circumstances who alone shows us what human life at its best can be like. He perhaps shows us what human *beings* at their best can be like, if we think of human beings in terms of their 'selves' or characters. We might even allow that a man who achieves great things morally has achieved *one* kind of *eudaemonia*, excellence along one possible dimension, as it were. I shall consider this possibility at the end of the section. But to assume that this is all there is to *eudaemonia* – that all that matters in human life is character – is to beg the question.

The fifth argument, or rather collection of arguments, derives from Kant: they rest on the allegedly *conditioned* status of the goodness of anything other than virtue (or, for Kant, the good will). The argument has two distinct forms. According to the first, everything other than the dutiful will is conditionally good in the sense that it may be associated with or lead to evil: thus a villain may be helped in his villainy by good qualities such as courage, intelligence or patience.[15] This argument seems to me confused. Firstly, the dutiful will itself seems to be conditionally good in the same sense; certainly people can be led to do evil by their very dutifulness. Kant would say that this is ruled out by his specification of the 'form of law itself' as that to which the dutiful will is obedient. But notoriously his principle of universal law has insufficient content to proscribe many actions which would normally be thought of as bad. More importantly, to show that something is in this sense conditionally good is not to show that it is not good in itself. Why should we not say that the villain's deeds are all in all wicked but nevertheless contain an ingredient which as far as it goes is good, namely the exercise of a fine human quality?

The second Kantian argument, implicit in Kant's thought rather than stated, rests on his belief that only when a person is acting for the sake of duty is he autonomous; in all other cases he is determined by his desires. According to this argument, the good will is the only thing good in itself because it is the only expression of man's *autonomy*. This argument, however, really depends on an assumption that autonomy is the only thing good in itself, or perhaps that personhood, which for Kant might be said to consist in this autonomy, is the only thing of ultimate value. I shall discuss the notion of personhood as a criterion of the good in itself in a later section. It does not in any case yield the conclusion that the good will is the *only* thing good in itself, unless one makes various further assumptions, such as that the autonomous exercise of reason is the only thing valuable about a person and that man is determined, heteronomous, unless he is acting dutifully, both of which assumptions I would deny.

I conclude that none of these arguments for either version of the thesis that morality is the only thing good in itself is convincing. But it may still be felt that morality, even if not the only thing good in itself, cannot be regarded as simply one good among others; it is in some sense a supremely or incommensurably high good. This idea might however take one of several forms. It may simply be a confused version of the truism I have already noted, that no *action* can claim precedence over the morally *right* one. As we have seen, this fact need not show that moral rightness is good in itself at all, let alone of special status.

Secondly, the thesis might be that the improvement of one's

own moral *character* is always to be preferred to the acquisition of any other thing good in itself where a choice has to be made. The difficulty here is to think of a situation in which it would make sense to speak of having this kind of choice.[16] But one can imagine, for example, that a young and naïve artist from the country, offered the chance of studying in the city with all its opportunities both for development of talent and for corruption of morals, might see his decision as to what he ought to do (or be invited by his mentors to see it) as a choice *between* development of moral character and of creative talent.

The artist's dilemma assumes this form, however, only if he holds a very odd view of the nature of moral character. The usual view is that, although certain temptations may make it more difficult to retain one's character, it is always possible to do so. On this view, to abandon the scholarship because it brought one into temptation would be to abandon a good simply because it brought moral difficulties with it; and this is certainly not obviously right. And indeed if the artist says to himself, 'If I go to London I shall be corrupted', he is surely exhibiting *mauvaise foi*, the pretence to oneself that one is determined rather than a free agent.[17]

I suggest, then, that an agent logically cannot choose between his own moral development and the achievement of other goods, because he can always have moral development; and therefore we cannot construe the idea that virtue is a supreme good as implying that it is always to be chosen in preference to other goods. Of course it might make sense to speak of a possible conflict between promoting *other* people's moral character and promoting their talents. But in such cases we do not in fact seem to regard it as obvious that it is character which must always take precedence. For example, we might well think a parent mistaken, if he stopped a gifted child's music lessons because the child's success was making him conceited.

There is a third possible interpretation of the claim that morality is an incommensurably or supremely high good. This is the claim that no life, however full of other worthwhile things, can be thought of as worthwhile if its possessor does not retain virtue: 'What shall it profit a man, if he gain the whole world, and lose his own soul?' The idea is that no amount of other goods can compensate in value for the lack of virtue. As before, it is necessary to try to think of a case which would illustrate this point in practice. If a man already has all the other ingredients of *eudaemonia*, he can also have virtue if he wishes; so the question of a choice between virtue and everything else does not arise for him. It might arise, however, for someone whose circumstances are such that he feels he can get *eudaemonia* only at the price of doing something wrong. To anyone who holds the view that *leisure* is essential for *eudaemonia*, examples of such a situation are easy to imagine; a person easily might be so placed that he can get the money he needs for leisure for his worthwhile activities only by prostitution or large-scale fraud or other crime.[18] If to take the other extreme *eudaemonia* is seen as something which can be achieved in and through any ordinary work and social life, the situations where a man has to choose between it and duty will be rare. But a possible case would be that where a man's duty requires him to protest against a tyrannical régime even on pain of solitary confinement in prison or in a mental hospital.

Now it is clear (indeed, it is true by definition) that people with this kind of choice ought to choose to do their duty. But it is less clear whether we should say that such a man has sacrificed *eudaemonia* to duty, or whether we should rather maintain that a way of life which is contrary to duty cannot constitute *eudaemonia* in any case. I think that perhaps we have a choice here. If we concentrate on what a man does, rather than what he is, when speaking of his *eudaemonia*, it will seem natural to say that a man who as a result of doing his duty cannot do any of the things we have described as worthwhile has (rightly) sacrificed his *eudaemonia*. If on the other hand we think of *eudaemonia* as standing for a whole way of life embracing what a man *is* as well as what he does, we might say that if a man is not good 'in himself', his whole life is too tainted to be a 'good life'. Something might turn here on whether a man's worthwhile activities were 'bought' by one wicked act, now repented of, or whether they depend on a continuing defiance of what is seen by him to be a duty. In the latter case his whole character is poisoned; in the former case it need not be.

Note that if we choose to say that *eudaemonia* by definition cannot be had at the price of doing what is wrong, this does not *entail* that, if a man does do what is right, he thereby achieves *eudaemonia* whatever else he loses; this would follow only if one wanted to insist that *eudaemonia* must be possible to all men at all times. But it would make sense to maintain, as a *separate* thesis, that moral integrity is so important that if a man succeeds in holding on to that, he has achieved one form of worthwhile life, however impoverished and miserable his circumstances are in other ways.

This then is the fourth version of the thesis that virtue has a special status among goods. It is not the same as the thesis that virtue alone is good in itself. This latter, stronger, thesis would entail that a virtuous life could not be *improved*, however cramping and poor its circumstances, because it already contained all that is worth having. The thesis under discussion, however, would allow the possibility of degrees of *eudaemonia*. Thus the prisoner who resists the temptations of his captors amid appalling circumstances has, on this view, already achieved a piece of living sufficiently worthwhile to be called *eudaemonia*. But if he is set free and resumes his personal relationships and his scientific or artistic work, his life exhibits a fuller kind of *eudaemonia*: it is more worth having than his previous life, quite apart from its greater happiness.

There seems to be no particular difficulty in marking the admiration we feel for moral achievement by allowing it in this way to constitute a form of *eudaemonia* by itself, provided we also allow that there are better forms to be had where they are permissible and possible. This view would entail the conclusion that everyone is capable of some form of *eudaemonia*, if we make the assumption that moral goodness is possible for everyone. But it clearly would not entail that everyone is capable of the same degree of *eudaemonia*.

5   *Criteria for* Eudaemonia: *Intuition and Transcendental Deduction*

For the rest of the chapter I wish to consider the question of how one might *justify* a claim that something is worthwhile or good in itself and so forms a possible ingredient in *eudaemonia*. To do this I shall discuss various possible criteria which have been proposed in this connection, considering them largely in the light of the kinds of thing which people suggest as possible goods in themselves, such as aesthetic and scientific activity, the exercise of moral virtue, the cultivation of personal relationships. In a situation like this there is really a process of *mutual* justification: we appeal to our ideas of what is good in itself to test possible criteria, and we appeal to possible criteria to test our ideas of what is good in itself. This is a similar process to that undertaken in the search for a criterion of right action: we test possible criteria in the light of our 'intuitive' judgements as to what actions are right and wrong, and then, having established acceptable criteria, we review our piecemeal moral convictions in the light of them. This procedure might seem to be viciously circular. But I can escape this accusation of circularity if I depict my procedure, not as establishing *either* a criterion on the basis of piecemeal judgements *or* piecemeal judgements on the basis of a criterion, but as presenting criterion and judgements as a coherent whole, which is to carry persuasiveness partly by virtue of its very coherence.

It might be thought that the quest for such a criterion is a vain one: that whereas things good as means can be shown to be good by demonstrating that they are conducive to things good as ends, things good as ends must be taken to be so without proof.[19] This is not all that can be said on the subject, however. As well as those who say that we simply intuit that certain things are good in themselves, we have Mill's own 'considerations capable of determining the intellect' in favour of happiness as the only thing good in itself, we have attempts to establish a list of things good in themselves by a kind of transcendental deduction, and we have a kind of argument which I shall call a *redescription* argument.

It would be fair to say that G. E. Moore, among others, thought that we simply *intuit* what things are good in themselves.[20] He is of course keen to say that he is 'not an Intuitionist in the ordinary sense of the term', which he takes to refer to intuition of what actions are right, rather than of what things are good. But he is willing to say that one can use the term 'intuitions' of his propositions as to what things are good in themselves, meaning that we cannot prove such assertions to be true. He thinks that we all intuit in this way that 'personal affections and aesthetic enjoyments include *all* the greatest, and *by far* the greatest, goods we can imagine'.[21] One difficulty of such a view is of course that we do not all intuit this. From the beginning of Western philosophy many have given as high a place to intellectual endeavours and/or to contemplation of eternal verities. We may need in the end to say that there is simply irresolvable *disagreement* as to what the things good in themselves are; certainly the question is not as easily settled as Moore suggests. The second unsatisfactory aspect of an intuitionist account is that it yields an unconnected list of goods in themselves. Again, we may have to be satisfied with this, but it would be at least more theoretically economical if goods in themselves could be seen as linked by some common idea or feature, even if the basis for this is no less intuitionist than for the unconnected list of goods.

As I have said, Mill thought he could show, in a sense which fell short of proof, that happiness and happiness alone is good as an end.[22] This 'proof' is usually criticised on the grounds that it involves an illicit transition, from 'desired' to 'desirable'. Now it has indeed been the whole tenor of my thought that a thing is not desirable simply because it is desired. But Mill would be on stronger ground if he argued that a thing is desirable if it is the *only* thing which can be desired for itself. For to say that a thing is desirable must surely imply that it *can* be desired for itself; if a thing is the only thing desired for itself then either it is desirable or nothing is. Mill did of course think that happiness is the only thing which is desired for itself, and if he were right in this, it might be reasonable to maintain that happiness is the only thing desirable as an end. (It might be *more* reasonable to say that in that case *nothing* is desirable as an end, on the grounds that the point of the word 'desirable' would be lost if it could not be taken as commending some possible ends and not others.) But as we have seen, happiness is not the only thing desired as an end. Nor is the happiness which Mill speaks of in this passage *one* thing in any case, since it is a name for all the things desired for their own sakes.

In view of the limitations of the intuitive approach, there have been some attempts to follow a Kantian procedure and establish things as good in themselves by a form of transcendental deduction. This type of reasoning establishes not that we are right to value certain things but that we cannot help doing so, that certain things are necessarily regarded as valuable in themselves. There is thus a kind of subjectivity in this account of valuation. The necessity is located, not in the intrinsic valuableness of things themselves, but in the inevitable workings of our valuing minds. Perhaps there is no need to regret this, provided we can be convinced that the necessities are really *necessities* of our thought rather than contingent psychological tendencies and that they will yield a rich enough account of things good in themselves.

The two examples of transcendental deduction which I shall consider are, however, not entirely satisfactory on these counts. Firstly I shall mention the account of R. S. Peters in *Ethics and Education*.[23] He sees his list of things good in themselves, or worthwhile activities as they are in his account, as a list of possible answers to the practical question, 'Why do this rather than that?', and he thinks answers to this question can be derived by considering the presuppositions of practical discourse, to which the question belongs. He provides a justification of intellectual activities as follows: 'To ask the question "Why do this rather than that?" seriously is ... however embryonically to be committed to those enquiries which are defined by their serious concern with those aspects of reality which give context to the question which [a man] is asking.'[24] The activities which Peters mentions in this connection include 'science, literature, history and philosophy'.

Some criticisms of Peters's general method are developed by R. S. Downie and myself.[25] In the present context I should like to add a point which we do not make: an important limitation of Peters's procedure as he employs it (though less important in a book on education than it would be in a more general context) is that it yields (by most standards) a very truncated list of possible worthwhile activities. Thus even aesthetic activities can be included only in so far as they can be seen as forms of learning about the world and oneself. This may be relevant to the justification of the appreciation of literature and painting. But it would be very difficult to apply it to any *creative* aesthetic activity, and to the appreciation of non-representational art such as music (as Peters himself acknowledges).

Another transcendental deduction of things good in themselves is that of J. N. Findlay in his *Axiological Ethics*.[26] Findlay's deduction starts from what he sees as the essentially *public* nature of all language (not just practical discourse), and from there he goes on to argue that 'the entry into other people's, and into other sentient beings', feelings and interests is a necessary part of our experience of a possible world and of our ability to talk significantly and testably about it'.[27] This necessary tendency to put ourselves into others' shoes 'must' lead us to adopt a 'higher level of interest', in terms of which we desire and like only what everyone must desire and like. And 'some rising to this impartial standpoint is not only involved in all practical co-operation but also in the developed form of the discourse which goes with it'.[28]

As a result of this process, we are led to value 'universal pleasure and happiness' and then to value explicitly the impartiality (justice) which is implicit in the stance which abstracts from our own interests. Further, we come to value 'that imperfect but more intense rising above the specificity and particularity of interest which is involved in the deeper forms of unselfish personal love',[29] aesthetic and cognitive pursuits because 'they rise above the specificity and particularity of first-order interest',[30] and finally the 'moral value or virtue of pursuing all these variously specified values'.[31]

This line of argument is very attractive. But there are a great many gaps in it, even allowing for the fact that this account is only an outline. For one thing, it is necessary to distinguish between the publicness of language and impartiality. We must adopt a public stance in some sense if we are to use language at all. But a person who says 'It's nice', 'I like it', though using the public language, is not 'divesting himself of the specificity of his interest', and it is a further question how far people are committed to sometimes doing the latter. It is trivially true that sincere (that is to say, disinterested) counsel adopts a relatively impartial standpoint, and that requests for advice assume such an adoption. But how far *must* we counsel or seek counsel? And if we must, why *must* the impartiality concerned increase its scope until it includes everyone? It seems that there is in fact a psychological tendency, both in the history of moral thinking and in the history of any one individual, to widen the scope of those whose interests are thought to be relevant in deliberation as to what to do. But this is not the same as saying that we *necessarily* must come to form judgements in this way.

It might however be said that this fundamental line of criticism does not matter so much for our present purposes; if Findlay has shown that attaching ultimate value to personal relationships and to aesthetic and intellectual activity is a necessary consequence of subscribing to the principles of utility and justice, then we need not worry about whether he can transcendentally deduce these latter principles, since (we may suppose) they are not controversial in any case, and may be taken as given, however established.

But I am not convinced that Findlay can succeed even in this more modest aim. Presumably the reason why it is held that the man who values justice must value friendship is that in friendship disinterested concern for another person is displayed – and disinterestedness is the essence of justice. But although both friendship and justice transcend self-interest, they do so in opposite ways. Friendship is concern for one individual, whereas justice is concern for each individual equally. It might be said that friendship is a kind of microcosm of justice, in that it involves that kind of concern for one person which, if we are just, we have for everyone. But this is not the case, since friendship is concern for a particular individual because he is *that individual*, whereas justice is concern for individuals because they are human beings. It *may* be that justice requires us to have the same *degree* of concern for all as we have for our friends, but it cannot require the same *kind* of concern, which is by definition exclusive. In any case, in practice friendships and other personal relationships can be as much the enemies of justice as self-love. I should maintain that the lover of justice, *qua* lover of justice, is committed to an *ambivalent* view on friendship: approval of its disinterestedness, disapproval of its partiality.

The cases of intellectual and aesthetic activity are more complex. It might be maintained that both types of activity do have built into them a kind of impartiality, in that in their different ways what is aimed at is something which is to be valid for everybody. Thus the scientist, for example, aims to produce not just something which seems right to him, or which he personally is inclined to believe, but something which will be as it were true for everybody, resting on evidence or argument which will be agreed to be such by all. The layman who studies his work should be saying, not 'Does this fit my preconceptions?', or 'Would it be a convenient thing to believe?', but 'Is this shown to be true?' Again, the artist tries to produce something which is not merely satisfying to *his* whim but is in some way right or significant or valid for anyone, and the layman who tries to appraise and appreciate what he does hopes to get past 'knowing what he likes' to some notion of what *deserves* liking, or at least appreciation.

This kind of point is a good deal more controversial in the arts than in the sciences. Certainly I would not want to subscribe to a notion that there can be *rules* for good art, or even universalisable reasons why a good piece of art is good. I am thinking rather of such things as the tendency, which both the artist and his audience can have, to feel that some ways of finishing a work of art would be 'wrong' and others 'right'. There can however be *disagreement* in such aesthetic judgements, and then the question can be raised whether in the end it is simply a 'matter of taste', not to be disputed, or whether there is a 'right answer' in aesthetic matters. Indeed there are also branches of science, and ways of looking at science, of which it might be said that choice between theories is likewise a matter of taste. Findlay's transcendental deduction, however, requires that both art and science be seen as pursuits incorporating objectivity, at least in the sense of a theoretically possible agreement on truths and beauties which are so for all.

It can fairly be objected, however, that on this principle one can transcendentally deduce that playing cricket is ultimately valuable. For cricket is likewise an activity which is governed by principles which are the same for all, and in which the participants strive to respect the idea that a no ball is a no ball whoever bowls it, a stumping is a stumping whoever is out by it, and so on. If the only reason why those committed to justice and impartiality *must* favour art and science is that they are governed by impartial rules and considerations, then most activities with any kind of rule-governed structure will equally qualify.

Findlay's reply would have to be that there is for his purposes a radical difference between activities which are rule-governed, but of which the main point is something else, like cricket, and activities which are in some sense celebrations of rule-governedness or objectivity itself, like science. Whereas his transcendental deduction cannot justify playing cricket, or selling stocks and shares (though according to him it can justify fair dealings in both pursuits) it might be held to justify science, *if* the point of science is in the end to be regarded as the pursuit of objective truth itself; and similarly to justify art, if the point of art is the pursuit of objective aesthetic values.

There is something tempting about this idea, especially if one notes that it need not be given the quasi-Platonic tone that my language may suggest. The pursuit of truth or of beauty need not be the pursuit of a self-subsistent Platonic truth or beauty. But I shall not in the end espouse this method of justifying my suggested goods in themselves. For one thing, there is the controversy about whether aesthetic endeavour is to be seen in this objective fashion. But more fundamentally, I doubt whether the progress from impartiality in the consideration of people's interests (justice) to intellectual or aesthetic objectivity is as natural as Findlay suggests. Clearly there is some connection. But many people who are passionately concerned to promote *justice* would see no point in what I have been saying about art and science. Nor would one wish to accuse them of 'deep perversity', Findlay's name for the failure to take a step in his deductive process.

6   *Criteria for* Eudaemonia: *The Distinctive Human Endowment*

I turn now to another kind of attempt to justify ultimate values, by means of what I shall call a 'redescription' argument. The aim here is to show certain things to be good in themselves by redescribing them in terms of some embracing concept or idea which is already thought of as good in itself. This tactic does of course appeal to a basic value-judgement which is taken as axiomatic – a basic intuition, if you will. But it is perhaps more attractive to reason than the unconnected intuitions of the intuitionists whom I touched on earlier. I shall consider two redescription arguments: in this section that in terms of the distinctive human endowment, and in the following section that in terms of self-realisation (the latter resting to some extent on the idea of the distinctive human endowment, but including also other elements).

The phrase 'distinctive human endowment' is of course J. S.

Mill's;[32] he used it to denote those aspects of human personality the development of which, he thought, constituted 'utility in the largest sense',[33] the ultimate good on which (when he managed to get free of a narrower Benthamist account) his utilitarianism is based. The idea that there are some kinds of behaviour which are characteristic of a human being as opposed to a (lower) animal, and that this is the behaviour which is to be fostered and encouraged, runs through *Utilitarianism* as well as *On Liberty*: for example, it is crucial to the distinction between higher and lower pleasures.[34] But of course Mill did not invent the notion. We find something of the sort even in Kant, who speaks of 'the promotion of humanity as an end in itself' in terms of not neglecting the 'capacities for greater perfection which form part of nature's purpose for humanity in our person'[35] – a point where he seems to depart from his austere doctrine that 'morality, and humanity in so far as it is capable of morality, is the only thing which has dignity'. Its proper source, however, as Mill acknowledges,[36] is in Greek philosophy, and notably in Aristotle, who pursues the quest for the nature of *eudaemonia* by deciding what man's characteristic *ergon* is: the use of his reason.[37]

Before I give a more detailed account of Aristotle's conception of reason, I should like to pause to consider where precisely the basic intuition of value comes in. As is often pointed out, human beings differ from animals in many ways besides their use of reason. The question therefore arises how the specification of *reason* as the distinctive endowment in question is arrived at, and how far this selection is itself an evaluation. I think there are three possibilities here. Firstly, it might be suggested that reason is picked out because we *already* set a value on certain qualities and capacities in human beings, as the word 'endowment' suggests, and think these can all be embraced by the idea of reason. These would be the capacities signified by the words 'person', 'personality', where these are evaluative or partly so. On this view, our basic evaluation is of the form 'the exercise of reason is good in itself', and human beings are valued in a sense which derives from this. Secondly, it might be suggested that the basic value-intuition is that human beings as a species are uniquely valuable. The value we set on the activities of reason would then be derivative, and could be arrived at by a (relatively) value-*neutral* appraisal, as to what features about human beings made their lives so different from those of other animals. Thirdly, it might be suggested that the whole scheme of things ('Nature') is in some way good in itself, that each part of creation has its own role to fulfil in the general purpose, and that we ascertain this role in the case of each species by seeing what activity would not be performed if that species did not exist – this decision as before being seen as relatively value-neutral.

It is of course very difficult in practice to assign the thought of an author exclusively to one of these positions; but I imagine that it could plausibly be argued that Aristotle adheres implicitly to the third, Mill to the second, and Kant to the first without always distinguishing it from the second. For my present purposes, however, the differences between these positions need not matter too much. Whether the basic value-judgement exalts reason, human beings or the purposes of creation, the things which we can ourselves promote and foster are at the level of characteristic human activities. Discrepancies between the positions at the level of what we can *do* would arise only if it transpires that what can be established, in the comparatively value-neutral, quasi-biological style of Aristotle, to be the characteristic activity of man differs in content from what adherents of the first position would value directly. To see whether this might be so, let us now turn to Aristotle's account.[38]

Aristotle begins by saying that man exhibits 'the life of nutrition and growth', but this cannot be his characteristic activity, since he shares this even with plants. Next he mentions the life of sentience which distinguishes man from plants, but this is shared by animals also. Finally he comes to the life of reason, which only man exhibits. This can be subdivided in various ways. We can distinguish within it that which reasons and that which is subservient to reason (by the latter he means emotions and in general what later writers would call 'passions'). That which reasons, or reason proper, can be subdivided into practical and theoretical branches, and the practical branch can be subdivided into that concerned with means to ends and that concerned with the kind of action which is an end in itself.

Now if all activities manifesting the use of reason, in all these subdivisions, are to be considered worthwhile in themselves, then it might fairly be said that most human action falls under that description, and the whole concept is a meaningless one. But in fact Aristotle has two further conditions: firstly the rational activity in question must be a *good* performance of its kind, exhibiting the relevant virtues,[39] and secondly it must be something which can be valued for its own sake.[40] In the end he allows only two candidates for constituents of *eudaemonia*: contemplation, and the exercise of moral virtue.[41] The relationship between these two is a little problematic, and some commentators write as though contemplation is *the* recommended activity and regard for moral virtue only the condition under which it is to be performed: 'a rational activity in accordance with virtue'. But whereas Aristotle says that his contemplators have to be morally virtuous,[42] the virtue which would most closely be connected with contemplation would be an *intellectual* one (though not one of those he lists, which concern skill in *attaining* the truth) and the activities in which moral virtue is most signally shown are supposed to be those of the man of affairs, the politician or soldier.[43] Moreover, he allows that those not capable of contemplation are nevertheless capable of achieving a lower form of *eudaemonia* in so far as they practise moral virtue.[44]

The first point which strikes the reader in this account is the stress on *contemplation* of the truth, rather than on rational enquiry; it is not at first clear why he mentions one and not the other. The reason must be that he sees research as a means to the end of discovering truth, and so not valued for its own sake. But, as we saw earlier, the fact that an activity is directed towards an end need not mean that its whole value is an instrumental one. It would make sense to maintain that a period of time spent in research was time well spent, even though nothing came out of it; and some people would want to allow for this.

The Aristotelian can say here, however, that Aristotle could have allowed for this point within his own basic scheme, in terms of his dictum that an exercise of a virtue, whether intellectual or moral, is a good in itself.[45] It is true that he defines the intellectual virtues as various kinds of capacity for arriving at the truth, but if one were to refine this and say that an intellectual virtue is a capacity which enables a man to arrive at the truth 'most of the time', or 'more often than not', or 'more often than most people', one could then go to depict the good scientist's year exploring a blind alley as worthwhile because it was an exercise of the intellectual virtues, even though this time they did not 'pay off'.

There remain two values connected with intellectual life which Aristotle does not incorporate, but which some people (different people in the two cases) would wish to allow for. One is eliminated, not by Aristotle's basic insistence on reason as the basis of *eudaemonia*, but by his insistence that the final good shall be an *activity* rather than a state. For even someone who takes the point that research need not be seen as an activity which is only instrumentally valuable might still want to say that the *main* value of it lies in its conduciveness to particular intellectual *states* of mind, in the researcher and later in those who learn about his research: namely, increased knowledge and understanding. Of course knowledge and understanding show themselves in action in various ways. But, all the same, there is a difference between the state of possessing knowledge and the activity of contemplating what is known; and those who agree with Aristotle that reason is the basis of *eudaemonia* might nevertheless differ from him when he says that only contemplation can be good in itself.

The other aspect of intellectual good is ruled out by Aristotle's stipulation that *eudaemonia* shall consist in *virtuous* rational activity, rather than in rational activity as such. I said earlier that the scientist's abortive research might be allowed to be valuable in itself by Aristotle if it can be seen as an exercise of intellectual virtue. But some would say that intellectual enquiry could be valuable in itself even if it is muddle-headed and misguided, on the principle that if a thing is worth doing it is worth doing badly. They hold, in other words, that the exercise of the intellectual faculties is always a good thing in itself because it is a manifestation of the capacity which distinguishes human beings from animals. This would be the thinking behind the attempt to get even children of very low intelligence to do academic work of a kind, rather than confine them to acquiring practical skills; to show that these children are not achieving understanding or knowledge as a result of the process would not necessarily condemn it, according to this point of view.

Three brief comments on this idea must suffice. Firstly in its favour one might point out that there is a difference between saying that someone is good *at* exercising a certain capacity and saying that the exercise of it is a good thing; Aristotle is perhaps too ready to assume that a person who has secured the good for man or *eudaemonia*, what is worth having in life, must be a person who is good *at* characteristically human life. Secondly, in anticipation of obvious practical criticisms of the view, it can be pointed out that to hold that incompetent intellectual activity is a good in itself is not to deny that competent intellectual activity has a much greater value from an instrumental point of view, in terms of the resulting knowledge of the practitioner and others, and is therefore *more* valuable overall, other things being equal, since great instrumental value can outweigh small intrinsic value, as we said, and competent intellectual activity has intrinsic value as well. Thirdly and damagingly, it can surely be asked whether there does not come a point where incompetent intellectual enquiry ceases to be intellectual enquiry at all. If people have *no* understanding of what they are doing, then it is no longer clear that we have a case of exercise of the theoretical intellect at all, rather than a display of what Mill called 'the ape-like faculty of imitation'.[46]

I turn next to the practice of morally virtuous activity, which has of course been depicted by many philosophers as in one way or other a paradigmatically rational activity. Aristotle connected moral virtue with reason in two ways: moral virtue depends on the possession of an intellectual virtue, *phronesis* or practical wisdom, which tells its possessor how to act virtuously in a given particular case; and the moral virtues themselves are seen as the tempering or balancing of natural tendencies to emotion until an appropriate balance or *mean* discerned by practical wisdom is achieved, in other words as modes of rationality in Aristotle's 'obedience to reason' sense. In this way Aristotle can readily show how his general formula, good rational activity, can justify regarding moral virtue as part of *eudaemonia*.

Nowadays we are perhaps inclined to think of the value of the

moral virtues in terms of their usefulness to others, rather than
of their rationality; or we might, with Kant, fuse the two
conceptions, and depict the rationality of morality as consisting
in obedience to a law valid not only for oneself but for all. But
from the point of view, not of morality seen as essentially
interpersonal, but of *eudaemonia* or individual welfare, we can
understand Aristotle's portrayal, not only of such other-
regarding virtues as generosity, but also of qualities like courage and tenacity which need not concern others at all, as
exemplifying an ideal of obedience to reason. In fact, *pace* Kant,
we can allow even 'the coolness of a villain' to be good in itself
although the deed exhibiting it is an unjust one.

The trouble with this line of thought, however, is that it
seems to justify too much. If part of what makes moral virtue
reasonable for Aristotle is the exercise of the virtue of practical
wisdom which discerns where virtue lies, why should we not
say that the exercise of the virtue of *techne* – skill in finding
means to ends – as shown for example by the good engineer, is
good in itself as well? Aristotle would doubtless say that such
activities are not valued for their own sakes, since they are
directed towards an end. But, as we saw before, Aristotle is
wrong here; we can *abstract* from the end in view and regard
such examples simply as cases of skilful rational behaviour. If
Aristotle wants to maintain that moral virtue is rational in a
sense in which practical cleverness is not, he would have to say
that reason tells us, not only what constitutes virtue in a given
case, but also that it is the only ultimate end or that we should
aim at it – a kind of Aristotelian equivalent to the Kantian
authoritativeness of the categorical imperative relative to the
hypothetical.

But even more drastically it might be asked, for example by a
disciple of Mill, whether there is not something valuable in the
mere process of working out what to do and doing it. Whether
or not moral or intellectual *virtue* is shown, here we have, it
might be said, a paradigm case of practical reason, part of the
characteristic human endowment, at work; and this activity is
therefore worthwhile in itself. Mill certainly writes sometimes
as though the activity of making deliberate choices in life, as
distinct from the ape-like imitation of drifting with the herd, is
worthwhile no matter what is chosen, and so gets himself into

problems about what to say if what is rationally chosen is non-rational or counter-rational. Perhaps from the point of view of articulating the conception of reason as the characteristic endowment one can agree that the faculty of choice is valuable in itself and to be cherished, but go on to say that this dictum is only a minimal statement of the conception in question. It may give guidance on how to treat others, but it cannot by itself tell a man *what* choices to make where only his own life is concerned. This he must answer by considering which activities deploy reason *best*.

It may be thought that I have so stretched the conception of reason and rational activity as to exclude very little indeed. But besides excluding the drifting with the herd which Mill was concerned to castigate, even my stretched conception of reason also excludes attributes which, though they seem to belong to emotion rather than reason, might seem to some people an important part of what is worthwhile in itself in human life: intensity and spontaneity of feeling. This difficulty connects with another: that aesthetic activity and personal relationships, although often grouped with intellectual and moral activity as though forming part of the activity of the characteristic human endowment, are not very happily depicted as primarily activities of reason. I shall say a little about each of these types of activity in turn.

Aristotle notoriously does not mention aesthetic activities at all when listing candidates for *eudaemonia*, and it may be that he classed them as 'amusements' – activities which people do in fact undertake for their own sakes, but which should more properly be valued only as means to an end – aids to relaxation, which enable one to work again.[47] This seems to us quite inadequate as an account of art. But it is not clear how far we can correct Aristotle on the basis of his own premises and bring aesthetic activities under the umbrella of Reason. We can however say that the creative artist embodies in his work a plan or *design*, and that interpreting or appreciating his work involves the attempt to understand it, or grasp this design. We can also suggest, as I did earlier, that aesthetic appreciation involves a quest for rationality in the sense of interpersonal objectivity: good art is not just 'what I like' but what is worthy of appreciation or intrinsically lovable.

All this seems a little unsatisfactory, however. For one thing, this kind of account does not seem to suit the contemplation of beauty in *nature*, as distinct from art. But this activity would often be thought to be the most worthwhile of all. More generally, the account seems too intellectualistic, at least to suit appreciation. What is characteristic of our reactions to art, and to beauty in nature, is not only a sense of design or order but also an intensification of feeling. It does not matter whether we think (with Aristotle, on one interpretation) that the *after-effect* is a kind of draining away of emotion,[48] or whether we feel that the result is rather an increased sensitivity; at the time there is a sense of excitement and elation for which perhaps 'joy' is the best word.

To attempt to justify aesthetic activities in any way which leaves out this feature is to distort their nature. But it is more difficult to explain *why* joy is a justifying feature, since it seems to be a species of pleasure: one cannot justify aesthetic activities from the point of view of *eudaemonia* (though one could from the point of view of happiness) merely by saying they *are* enjoyed in a particular way. Perhaps the best manoeuvre here is to question the distinction between rational appraisal of aesthetic objects and the emotional reaction of joy: aesthetic joy, it may be said, is that emotion which is necessarily aroused, at least in some measure, by something thought to be worthy of aesthetic appreciation, rather as a moral emotion is necessarily involved in a moral judgement.[49] We could then say that aesthetic joy is worthwhile in so far as it is part of the rational or quasi-rational activity of aesthetic appreciation.

Aristotle does discuss friendship at length,[50] but not as a separate candidate for *eudaemonia*. Either it is a means to an end, or it is for the sake of pleasure – presumably therefore having the status of an amusement – or, if it is friendship proper, it seems to be part of the exercise of moral virtue: friends love each other for their moral worth, and practise moral virtue to each other.[51] To us this seems the *negation* of a personal relationship, which involves caring for someone as an individual, and not necessarily for *any* clear reasons, still less for those reasons which would lead us to approve of anyone.[52] In this sense, then, friendship (to use the term for all properly personal relationships) might be said to be *non-rational*. As we saw earlier, it involves the capacity to transcend the bounds of self, but not in any way which involves the true impartiality of reason. I suggest then that friendship cannot be justified in terms of the 'characteristic human endowment', if this is seen as comprising various modes of rational human activity.

If this is so, we are left with three possibilities. Either we must cease to claim that friendship is one of the things which is worthwhile in itself; or we must depict the things worthwhile in themselves as *mostly* describable in terms of rational activity, and add friendship as an unconnected extra; or we must find a richer way to describe the characteristic human endowment, a way which enables us to connect friendship with the other elements we have attributed to it. The first alternative is much at variance with many value judgements; the second is intellectually uneconomical and untidy; so we should explore the third possibility.

One way of linking friendship to the other suggested goods, suggested by the transcendental deduction we discussed earlier, is in terms of *imagination*. Friendship, it might be said, is a way of putting oneself in someone else's shoes, of living partly in someone else's experiences, and so on. Through friendship we *identify* with someone else, not merely in the sense that we intellectually adopt an interpersonal stance, but in a stronger sense: we acquire some acquaintanceship with what it is like to be that other person. But when friendship is described in this way it is seen to link with aesthetic activities. For in many of these – notably in the creation, appreciation and, where relevant, interpretation of literature – what is involved is the imaginative adoption of another individual's point of view. (This, for Plato, was precisely what was *bad* about it.) [53] In fact, we could depict some aspects of morality this way also, in terms of the rule not of reason but of *sympathy*. The 'characteristic endowment', then, becomes the capacity to exercise theoretical and practical reason and imagination, and the activities and states which traditionally are thought of as good in themselves – intellectual enquiry, understanding, aesthetic creation and contemplation, the exercise of moral virtue and the practice of friendship – can all be brought under these overlapping ideas.

7   Eudaemonia *and Self-Realisation*

I turn finally to the ideas of self-realisation and self-
development, which it might seem natural to invoke in connection with *eudaemonia*.[54] It is perhaps worth saying at the outset
that to describe the good for man in terms of self-realisation is
not to be committed to a *selfish* philosophy. I say this, not
because I wish to espouse a Bradleian doctrine that the true self
is a 'social self', which breaks down the distinction between self
and others, but because it is possible to hold that *eudaemonia* can
be seen in terms of self-realisation without committing oneself
to the view that a person's only business in life is to seek this for
himself, as opposed, say, to fostering it in others.

The concept of self-realisation is not, however, very helpful
as a redescription in terms of which activities can be shown to
be good in themselves. In some uses it seems more concerned
with *hedonistic* happiness: to realise *oneself* is to realise as many as
possible of one's desires, and the best method of doing this is to
try to harmonise them into a mutually reinforcing pattern.
Where self-realisation is concerned with what ought to be
wanted as distinct from merely what *is* wanted, in other words
with a man's 'better self' in some sense of that term, we need
some criterion for distinguishing what elements in a person
constitute his better self, and this brings us back to the characteristic human endowment.

But surely, it will be said, the concept of self-realisation if it is
to be of any use is to do with what is individual, rather than
what is generic – with what we may call the *idiosyncratic* self?
This is certainly part of what the term 'self-realisation' suggests; but in so far as it does this, it is not clear how far it still
offers a persuasive redescription in terms of which pursuits can
be justified as good in themselves. Is it obvious that someone
should develop a talent or capacity, or pursue an inclination,
which is his to a special degree, unless it is also worthwhile on
grounds other than that it is peculiarly his own? It is true that
Mill seems to lay great importance on the development of
individuality. But this seems to be, not a good in itself, but a
means to the deployment of the characteristically human endowment of the capacity for choice and decision. If a man is
being original, this shows that he must be choosing rather than

drifting; and if he is like everyone else, this is also acceptable, so long as he chooses to be so.[55]

Does the term 'self-development' add nothing to my conclusion to date, that the activities which make up *eudaemonia* can be 'redescribed' as manifestations of the characteristic human endowment, seen in terms of reason and imagination? On the contrary, the natural tendency to employ the idea of individual self-development in connection with *eudaemonia* points to three possible features of it which, while not in conflict with the broadly Aristotelian picture which I have so far drawn, tend to be ignored by it – three ways in which an individual's *eudaemonia* might be said to be *his* good and not merely a good life led by him.

The first feature is the possibility of individual *styles* of *eudaemonia*. Aristotle mentions only the intellectual who contemplates and the man in the street who practises moral virtue. But there could be *many* different ways of life which are all worthwhile in terms of the manifestations of the characteristic human endowment which I have discussed. To say that a certain kind of activity is worthwhile is not to say that every worthwhile life must contain it in equal measure, or at all. Perhaps, for example, some dedicated scientists or artists need to eschew personal relationships in order to practise their own worthwhile activity. On the other hand, someone might see his chief worthwhile activity as the cultivation of personal relations. Or again, *eudaemonia* for someone else might be the achievement of activities in all these fields. We might see a man's style of *eudaemonia* as in some sense '*given*' by his individual nature and opportunities, so that the question, 'What is *eudaemonia* for X?', is as objective as the question, 'What is *eudaemonia* as such?', or we might see the question of style as a question of the individual's choice of an ideal.

The second feature is the possible difference between individuals in capacity for *eudaemonia*. It would seem that an individual's capacity for achieving *eudaemonia* must vary enormously, in accordance with variations both in talents and in opportunities. Even allowing that *eudaemonia* is different for different people, it still seems possible to say that a person of rich talents and many opportunities can lead a life which is far more worthwhile, in the relevant sense, than that of someone who is very poorly endowed intellectually and has no cultural or personal opportunities. (This conclusion presupposes that we *can* draw a difference of value between intellectual activity manifesting a high degree of what Aristotle would call intellectual virtue and that which does not show any at all.) It is true that I suggested earlier that *everyone*, *qua* moral agent, can acquire that form of *eudaemonia* which is constituted by high moral achievement. But, as I made clear then, there can be degrees of *eudaemonia*. A man of high talent and great opportunities can achieve a higher degree of it than a man whose only asset is his capacity for morality.

The third feature of *eudaemonia* to which use of the term 'self-realisation' might draw attention is that the chance to achieve it might be seen as an individual's *right* or due, and one which might conflict with that of others no less than the right to the pursuit of hedonistic happiness. Again, this notion presupposes that there are degrees of *eudaemonia*, and that its highest forms consist of more than the opportunity to be virtuous – a good which no one can take from me or even diminish my share of. If this is true, and the pursuit of *eudaemonia* at its richest requires the provision of cultural, intellectual and social opportunities, then clearly issues of equity of distribution and conflict of interest can arise, since these things are not in unlimited supply.

3 The Relation between *Eudaemonia* and Hedonistic Happiness

1 Eudaemonia *as Necessary for Hedonistic Happiness*

So far I have written as though *eudaemonia* and hedonistic happiness are entirely distinct notions, while constantly hinting that they are related in various ways. In this chapter I propose to explore the relationship between the two concepts and to consider the question whether a situation can arise in which a man may be said to have to *choose* between his *eudaemonia* and his hedonistic happiness.

As has already been said, the difficulty is to show how *eudaemonia* is to do with *happiness* at all without collapsing it into hedonistic happiness. We can of course show, as I suggested in chapter 2, how *eudaemonia* in some way pertains or belongs to the individual, if for each person there exists an ideal form of *eudaemonia* which best uses his talents or which he chooses to espouse and so makes his own, and if each individual may have some rights in respect of his *eudaemonia* and some risk of competing with others in pursuit of it. But these considerations do not of themselves entail that *eudaemonia* is conducive to its possessor's happiness: that is, his hedonistic happiness.

It is tempting to say here that the question is whether *eudaemonia* benefits or profits its possessor, is in his interests or for his good or welfare. But we cannot approach the question *via* these notions without ambiguity, since as we saw in chapter 2 they all have a dual character. In one sense they are indeed connected with hedonistic happiness, and stand for what a person wants, or would want to hold on to if he once got it ('really wants'), or what (whether or not he knows it) will bring him what he wants. It is meaningful to ask whether *eudaemonia* profits a person in this sense. In the other sense, however, it would be empty, since in the second sense these terms are more or less *equivalent* to *eudaemonia*, and stand for what is worth wanting, what a person ought to want, what would make his circumstances or character better in terms of a standard other than merely that of what he wants.

As we saw in chapter 2, there are those who maintain that this distinction cannot be sustained, because they hold that there is no way of making sense of the objective valuation presupposed by talk of 'what a man ought to want' and so on, except in terms of what he does want. I dealt with this view at that point. But there is also the possibility of maintaining that in practice the distinction does not matter, since people must always want, or at any rate 'really want', the same things that they ought to want. It is this latter kind of view, which connects *eudaemonia* necessarily with hedonistic happiness without dissolving the distinction between them, which I wish to explore in this chapter.

There are various possible versions of the view: for example, it might be maintained either that *eudaemonia* is a necessary condition of hedonistic happiness or that it is a sufficient condition. Again, the connection may depend on the possessor of *eudaemonia* recognising it as such, or it may depend on the empirical nature of the ingredients which go to make it up. Thus it may be claimed that a man is hedonistically happy, or maximally so, if, or only if, he experiences in his life friendship, aesthetic experiences, and so on, and that this is because of the empirical nature of these things, perhaps their capacity to fulfil basic needs. Alternatively, it may be claimed that a man is hedonistically happy if, or only if, he can *regard* his life as worthwhile or objectively valuable. I now turn to an exploration of these possibilities.

The most plausible thesis in this connection might seem to be that a man cannot be hedonistically happy unless he regards his life as constituting a case of *eudaemonia*: in other words, that to possess *eudaemonia*, recognised as such, is a necessary condition for hedonistic happiness. Now it is true that if a man *has* an idea of the worthwhile life, in the *eudaemonia* sense, and moreover sets great store by exemplifying it as an ideal in his own life, then he will be unhappy if he fails to do so, whether the failure is through lack of opportunity or of effort. Indeed, this much follows from the definition of hedonistic happiness. Similarly, if a man adopts as an ideal his own self-realisation, or the achievement of a way of life embodying the characteristic human endowment, he will not be entirely happy if he thinks his present life is contrary to that ideal – though this is a question of degree, and ideals are of their very nature something which a man might be happy, though not content, to be approaching rather than achieving.

But there seems no reason to say that everyone must have this kind of ideal. There is nothing incoherent in the notion that a man might divide his life into traditional duties owed to others and pleasures in which he pleases himself with no idea of objective values. If such a man thinks of trying to lead a worthwhile life, it will be in the sense only of a morally respectable life. We may suppose for the sake of argument that a man cannot be happy if he breaks his own moral principles too much. But if his moral principles do not refer to *eudaemonia*, and if he takes the view that the only other standards of value are those of pleasure, and if he keeps his principles and obtains his pleasures, he can perfectly well be happy without thinking of his life in terms of *eudaemonia* at all, and indeed without accepting that there is a coherent notion to which this term applies. Such a view was exemplified by the philosopher (a man I should judge to be happy) who once said to me something like this: 'I don't understand all this stuff in *Ethics and Education*[1] about *worthwhile activities*. I understand about moral principles, but apart from that I *like* doing philosophy and I *like* blondes, and as far as I'm concerned that's it'.

A follower of Mill might say that this man's attitude is impossible, at least to 'a being of higher faculties', who 'can never really wish to sink into what he feels to be a lower grade of existence'.[2] This unwillingness, says Mill, is best called

> a sense of dignity, which all human beings possess in one form or another, and in some, though by no means in exact, proportion to their higher faculties, and which is so essential a part of the happiness of those in whom it is strong, that nothing which conflicts with it could be, otherwise than momentarily, an object of desire to them.

Even this language, strong though it is, does not imply that *everyone* is unhappy unless he can see his life as a case of *eudaemonia*. And even if we accept Mill's assumption, that those with the greatest 'higher faculties' have also the strongest sense of dignity, it is not obvious that their sense of dignity must concern itself with the question of their 'grade of existence'. The self-respect standard is basically a self-selected one; a person like my philosopher might therefore not see his self-respect as at stake at all when choosing between the blondes and Beethoven.

There is, however, an objection of a logical kind which might be raised to my thesis that a man may be happy without regarding his own life as an instance of *eudaemonia*. It may be claimed that emotions and attitudes logically imply judgements that their objects possess a certain characteristic: thus *fear* implies the belief that the object of fear is dangerous, *pride* that the object of pride is creditable, and so on. The characteristic corresponding to being pleased (the objection continues) must be *goodness*; to be happy, or pleased with one's life, therefore implies thinking it to be good.

It is difficult to answer this objection briefly, since it implies a whole theory of the nature of concepts of the emotions. I could however begin by conceding that to be pleased does indeed imply regarding the object with which one is pleased as good. But this sense of 'good' is not the sense in which *eudaemonia* is the *good* life. The latter sense is an *objective* sense of 'good', as distinguished earlier, implying standards which go beyond the mere liking of the person using the term; whereas to say, 'That's good', of something with which one is pleased is as a rule only to put into an objective style of speech what is really an expression of one's own reaction. I say 'as a rule' because there are cases, as I pointed out in chapter 1, where a person is pleased with something because he thinks it will bring him something *else*. In this kind of case, which we may call being mediately pleased, some kind of objective judgement *is* pre-supposed, namely that the object of the pleasure will have the desired result. But being pleased with one's life is not a mediate pleasure of this kind.

The objectors might say that their examples suggest an objective model for all the judgements entailed by emotions and attitudes: thus 'I fear' implies, not merely 'This is frightening' (which is simply the objective-style way of expressing the subjective 'I am afraid of this'), but also 'This is *dangerous*', which suggests objective claims about the nature of what is feared.

But this is not very convincing. Firstly, a person can be afraid of what he knows is not dangerous (for example spiders); in his case 'I fear' does imply only 'This is frightening'. Even if we waive this point, and proceed as though *fear* always involved a belief claiming objectivity, there seems no reason to insist that all cases of being *pleased*, wanting to hang on to something, must similarly be *because* one believes that something is the case; the non-mediate cases are, on my view, simply cases of wanting to hang on to something. It seems then that the attitudes which are offered as analogies with being pleased as such, and which have objective implications, are really analogous only to the mediate cases of being pleased, and so no reason has really been offered for assuming that if a person is pleased with something he always makes an objective judgement about its goodness.

I conclude then that my thesis stands: a man need not consider his life to be a case of *eudaemonia* in order to be happy. It should however be noted that even if it were rejected, on the grounds that every man possesses in some form a conception of the worthwhile life in my sense and wants to live it, it would not follow that the actual possession of *eudaemonia* is a necessary condition of hedonistic happiness. For a man may wrongly think that his life constitutes *eudaemonia* if he has distorted ideas of what is worthwhile. But since his happiness depends only on the *belief* that his ideal is being realised, it would not be impaired by the fact that it is not.

It might now be suggested that the real connection between *eudaemonia* and happiness does not after all depend on the person's *thinking* that his life is a case of *eudaemonia*, but rather on the fact that the various ingredients of *eudaemonia* are, by their very nature, so uniquely satisfying that no one can be happy without partaking of them, or some of them. Stated in this way, however, this sounds like an *empirical* thesis: that people are not happy unless they partake of intellectual pursuits, and/or have personal relationships, and/or contemplate the beauties of art and nature. Moreover, it is not obvious that it is universally true, if construed in this way. I think that an attempt might however be made to turn it into a conceptual thesis, by making use of the notion of *boredom*.[3] It might be suggested, firstly, that no one can (logically) be happy if he is bored with life; secondly, that no one can (logically) avoid being bored with life unless for a reasonable part of his life his intellect and/or his imagination are strenuously engaged; thirdly, that the things which strenuously engage the intellect and/or the imagination are (by definition) the ingredients of *eudaemonia*.

Now the last proposition cannot be said to be true *by definition*. *Eudaemonia* is by definition the way of life which is .good in itself or worthwhile. If it consists in activities which strenuously engage the intellect and/or the imagination, this is because these are in fact the activities which are valuable in themselves, not because these are the only activities which could logically be good in themselves. In terms of our previous discussion we would therefore grant the last proposition, but as true 'by valuation', as it were, not by definition. The first proposition is probably acceptable also, if one considers that to be pleased with life, as opposed to merely acquiescing in it, involves positively wanting to hang on to it, whereas being bored with life seems to imply that a change would be welcome almost for its own sake.

The difficulty lies in the second contention, that no one can avoid being bored with life unless his intellect or his imagination are strenuously engaged. It may be the case that these conditions are *sufficient* for the removal of boredom (I shall consider shortly how far *eudaemonia* is a sufficient condition of happiness), but it is clear that they are not necessary, or not necessary for everyone. I have already hinted at a quite different feature which may be sufficient to stave off boredom: *variety*. Another feature of the same general kind would be *unexpectedness*. Both these are features, not of individual items in a life, but of the pattern of life taken as a whole. If a person finds his life, as a whole, interesting (the opposite of boring) his attention may be being held, not by any quality of the ingredients which make it up, but by one of these overall elements. Thus a housewife might reply to the question, 'Aren't you bored with your life?': 'Not at all. Plenty of things happen: lots of neighbours drop in; I go to the shops, you never know what you'll see or who you'll meet there; on Mondays there's the bingo; on Wednesdays there's the Bring and Buy evening . . . '

I am not of course saying that everyone would avoid boredom on such a diet. Nor would I deny that someone else, following ostensibly the same programme, might succeed in avoiding boredom in a radically *different* fashion: namely, by turning these trivia into worthwhile activities. What I am concerned to show is only that for some people a life without worthwhile activities might be interesting enough. And if this is so, the 'argument from boredom' fails to show that *eudaemonia* is necessary for hedonistic happiness.

2 Eudaemonia *as Sufficient for Hedonistic Happiness*

I suggested just now that even though partaking in the activities which make up *eudaemonia* is not a necessary condition of happiness, it might be a sufficient condition. This thesis might be argued for in either or both of two ways: it might be said that the activities characteristic of *eudaemonia* are all activities which necessarily bring people pleasure, or it might be maintained that to be able to regard one's life as a whole as a case of *eudaemonia* is something which is sufficient to make a person pleased with his life. I shall look at each of these strands in turn.

The ways in which enjoyment can be connected with worthwhile activities are in fact rather more complicated than the above formula would suggest. For example, it might be said that the possession of *eudaemonia* is a guarantee of enjoyment in the sense that unless a person happens to enjoy study or culture or friendship he will not be able to sustain them to the degree required for *eudaemonia*; all these things are difficult, and need the encouragement of enjoyment if they are to be successful. If this line of argument can be upheld, it would show that some degree of pleasure is needed as a *means* to the achievement of *eudaemonia*, and hence that anyone who does achieve it must have some enjoyment in his life. But to be guaranteed some enjoyment is not to be guaranteed happiness. In order to be happy, a man must be pleased with his life as a whole, and as we saw in chapter 1 he may not be pleased however much enjoyment he gets: if, for example, he has some major disappointment or dissatisfaction.

It might well be retorted, however, that this argument in any case distorts the connection between pleasure and the activities which are good in themselves. Study, culture and friendship are not things which some people *happen* to enjoy; they are essentially enjoyable. This thesis might be supported in terms of some idea of basic human *drives* or *motives*, to which these activities correspond: human beings, it may be said, crave not only food, shelter and sex, but also knowledge, beauty and companionship, and so they are bound to enjoy (want to prolong and foster) activities which satisfy these basic needs.

So far this thesis is again an *empirical* thesis, about 'universal human nature' or the like. Perhaps, however, it can be restated as a conceptual thesis, but in terms of faculties rather than drives. Let us recall that the activities good in themselves were originally distinguished as such with reference to a 'characteristic human endowment': in other words, they must by definition all involve the exercise of important human faculties. If we follow Aristotle in thinking that pleasure attends the unimpeded use of one's faculties,[4] we shall have built a conceptual bridge between *eudaemonia* and pleasure.

But this is too simple. For one thing, it is not clear that pleasure can be *defined* in terms of the unimpeded use of faculties, rather than in terms of wanting, as in chapter 1. It surely is not a mere contingency, but true by definition, that people want to go on with what they get pleasure from. Perhaps among the things we want to go on with is the unimpeded use of our faculties, but this does not seem to be analytic. But more importantly we should note that Aristotle says '*unimpeded* use of faculties'. In real life the activities which are good in themselves are beset with 'impediments': experiments go wrong, or books and lectures are incomprehensible; one's painting does not manage to embody one's idea, or worse, does embody one's idea which then does not seem worth embodying; the music which everyone else seems to enjoy, and which one used to enjoy oneself, suddenly seems insipid, or one becomes discriminating in music and then is condemned to work to Muzak all day; friends turn indifferent, or die, or stay around and suddenly become unlikeable. All these things happen, and all of them can cause great distress. It may well be that *unimpeded* faculties and *satisfied* drives bring pleasure; but it is a doubtful question whether partly impeded faculties and partly thwarted drives bring more pleasure on balance than if the faculties are left undeveloped and the drives dormant. Moreover, the answer to the question will be different for each individual, depending on his talents and circumstances and also on his luck. No general answer is possible on this basis to the question of how far *eudaemonia* produces pleasure.

It might still be objected, however, that the connection between *eudaemonia* and pleasure is closer than has so far been allowed for. In my account just now of the frustrations of the seeker after *eudaemonia* I included failures as well as successes, and described the ingredients of *eudaemonia* as broad areas of endeavour. But it might be said that what is really worthy of the status of 'ingredient of *eudaemonia*' is only the successful or relatively successful performance of the types of activity in question. Thus for example friendship, properly so-called, is a relationship with a person who is neither dead nor indifferent nor uncongenial; this is what is said to be worthwhile, and the hazards encountered in the *quest* for it are irrelevant. And (the objector continues) this friendship, once achieved, *is* enjoyable; and this is not a mere contingency. Rather friendship *is* or involves the enjoyment of another's company. Similarly it might be argued that aesthetic contemplation *is* the enjoyment of the beautiful; and so on. The objector might even go so far as to say that the so-called *activities* which are good in themselves are really various good forms of *pleasure*.

The thesis in its extreme form can I think be rejected, on the grounds that, if value is being attached, not to pleasure as such, but to specific cases of it, this must be in virtue of a difference in the value of the *source* of the pleasure; in other words, the 'good forms of pleasure' presuppose the goodness of that in which the pleasure is taken. But a weaker form of the thesis, to the effect that pleasure is a necessary *part* of the account which must be given of each of the ingredients of *eudaemonia*, is perhaps less easy to dismiss. It seems natural to say that friendship *must* involve the enjoyment of each other's company. Again, as we saw earlier, a kind of pleasure seems to be built into the idea of aesthetic appreciation.

But can the same kind of move be made with all the ingredients of *eudaemonia*? For example, creative artists often enjoy their work, but it is not obvious that enjoyment is 'built in', in the sense that we should want to say that a creative artist who did not enjoy his work was no true artist, or that his

activity was not good in itself for this reason. The same is true of
the scholar or researcher.

The position of morality with regard to this issue is notoriously controversial. Aristotle, for example, held that enjoyment
of the practice of virtuous activity was a sign that the genuine
virtuous disposition had been achieved.[5] Kant, on the other
hand, thought that enjoyment was quite irrelevant to the
question of moral virtue and was inclined to suggest that virtue
is most signally present when the virtuous activity is against the
grain.[6] For Aristotle, then, pleasure is built into an account of
this particular activity good in itself, for Kant not.

Without wishing to accept the full austerity of the Kantian
position, I would argue that Aristotle is far too extreme here.
His view is plausible when applied to dispositions such as
kindness. But he himself was prepared to make an exception for
courage,[7] and there would surely be other cases where he would
have to admit that virtue consists in doing something which it
would be *wrong* to find pleasant: for example, giving up a friend
to the police. How much pleasure the life of virtue brings will
depend on what particular things a man is called upon to do:
one could not say that the virtuous life is necessarily a pleasant
one. And there are some *sorrows* which are necessarily built into
it: sorrow at others' sufferings, for example, is required by the
virtue of compassion.

I conclude that it cannot be argued that all the ingredients of
eudaemonia are by definition pleasurable. But even if we were
able to maintain this, it still would not follow that a life of
eudaemonia is always a happy life. For, as we saw earlier, a happy
life is not the same as a life of many pleasures. It must also be a
life free from major dissatisfactions. And it would certainly be
possible for a man to lead a worthwhile life, and enjoy those
aspects of his life which made it worthwhile, but still suffer from
a dissatisfaction sufficiently grave to spoil his happiness.
Perhaps, for example, he has always wanted a happy family life
and this escapes him; or he wants a public recognition of some
kind (say, a knighthood), craving for which unsettles him. Such
a man may have *eudaemonia*, but he does not have happiness.
The same kind of point can be made in reply to the argument
that the man with *eudaemonia* must be happy because he must be
pleased with his life as a whole if he sees it to constitute

eudaemonia: it may be that a man is bound to be pleased to think that his life constitutes *eudaemonia*, but if there is some important dissatisfaction then he will not be pleased with his life as a whole.

3   Eudaemonia *as Itself Implying Hedonistic Happiness*

So far the arguments I have considered which attempt to make the possession of *eudaemonia* sufficient for happiness have all built on the previous account of *eudaemonia* and tried to show how happiness necessarily arises out of it. But a quite different line of approach could be tried: namely, a thesis that no one's way of life could be called a case of *eudaemonia* unless it makes him happy, whatever ingredients it may contain. Instead of giving an account of *eudaemonia* in terms which do not include happiness and then asking whether *eudaemonia*, so described, does produce happiness, the new line of argument would start from a value-judgement that part of what makes a life good in itself in the first place is that it is a happy life. This line of thought thus attributes an objective value to pleasure, or at least to being pleased with one's life, since by definition an ascription of *eudaemonia* is an ascription of objective value. It also gives an extremely *high* objective value to it, in so far as it is being argued that no amount of worthwhileness in a life can make up for the lack of this one worthwhile element of happiness.

It is tempting to say here that it is obvious that a life is not really worthwhile unless it is a happy life. But the sense in which this is obvious is not the relevant one. It is analytic that one cannot on *prudential* grounds (grounds concerning what will produce happiness) recommend a life which is not a happy life. But one cannot assume that an unhappy life is not worthwhile in the sense of not *worth* wanting without begging the question at issue of the objective value of pleasure and in particular of happiness.

It might be objected here that the idea of pleasure's having an objective value at all is a contradiction in terms: surely pleasure is of its essence a matter of taste, or of subjective value. But this objection embodies a confusion. It is true that to take pleasure in or get pleasure from a thing may itself be regarded as a kind of subjective valuation, and as I said a person can say, 'That's good', of something, meaning only that he likes it or that it gives him pleasure. But this subjectiveness is quite compatible with setting an objective value on pleasure: one can consistently say that it is good, in some kind of objective sense, that people should have what they find good in the subjective sense involved in pleasure. And this is indeed what many schools of thought would wish to maintain. From what I have just said, then, it looks as though pleasure might be a possible good in itself and constituent of *eudaemonia*, alongside aesthetic and intellectual activities and friendship.

This idea can seem at first to embody a kind of category mistake: how can pleasure be put *alongside* aesthetic activities and so on, when these are the kinds of thing which can *give* pleasure? (This is the same kind of puzzlement that one has when first reading Plato's *Philebus*, in which there is a debate as to whether pleasure or reason is the best thing in life.) It is of course true that pleasure is in a different category from everything else, and it would be odd to say, 'Her life was worthwhile because it contained friendship, scholarship and pleasure' – odd at least if what is meant is that the pleasure is *gained from* the friendship and scholarship. But if one redescribes the situation so that the goods in themselves are seen as criteria for the worthwhileness of a life, rather than separable items in it, then pleasure seems to be able to take its place: 'the life of an Oxford Fellow is worthwhile because it is intellectual, personal, and pleasant.' (In a similar way, we can compare pleasure and reason, as in the *Philebus*, as possible criteria for *assessing* a life[8] – should a way of life be chosen in proportion to its pleasantness or to its intellectuality?)

There seem to be three ways of regarding the claim that pleasure is good in itself. The first view, which we may call Aristotelian, [9] would involve only a minor development of the account hitherto given of *eudaemonia*. According to this view, pleasure reflects the value of its source. If something is good, then enjoyment of it is a good state of mind, just as desire for it is good. If something is bad, then it is bad to desire or to enjoy it. According to this view then, the pleasure we take in activities good in themselves is itself good, and to be pleased with a life constituting *eudaemonia* would be a good kind of happiness. But this view would not entail the proposition that unless a man is pleased with his life it cannot constitute *eudaemonia*, since this view makes the value of the happiness depend on the value of the life, rather than *vice versa*: in other words, on this view we call the man's happiness good because we have already decided on other grounds that his life constitutes a case of *eudaemonia*.

The second sense in which pleasure might be said to be good in itself is of course the ordinary sense, characteristic of utilitarianism, according to which pleasure from *any* source, the mere fact of someone's getting what he likes, is something to be promoted and fostered. In traditional utilitarianism pleasure is the only thing to be valued in this way, but it is perfectly possible to hold that pleasure as such is good in itself but not the only such good.

The traditional objection to the view that all pleasure is good in itself is to quote examples of which it seems natural to disapprove: for example, pleasure at another's pain. If pleasure is held to be the only thing good in itself, this disapproval has to be accounted for by saying that the pain incurred by the sufferer must outweigh the pleasure enjoyed by the other, and that the total situation is bad only because of this preponderance of pain. But this reply would not explain why pleasure is held to be bad in those situations where there is no actual pain but someone is pleased because he believes there is.[10] If pleasure is not held to be the *only* thing good in itself, however, the difficulty can be avoided. One might say, for example, that the total situation is a bad one, because the goodness of the pleasure, as pleasure, is outweighed by the viciousness of taking pleasure in that particular thing.[11] We can therefore say that all pleasure is good in itself without being committed to the view that all instances of someone's enjoying himself are equally valuable.

In his *Foundations of Ethics*,[12] W. D. Ross argues that, although there is a sense in which pleasure is good in itself, it cannot be the same sense as that in which intellectual and artistic and moral activity are good in themselves. He allows that it must be good in itself in the sense that others' pleasure is a 'fit object of satisfaction' for a moral agent, and something which he has a *prima facie* duty to promote in general. But he maintains that pleasure is not good in itself in his strongest sense, for several reasons: we have no duty to promote the *bad* pleasure of others; a man is called a good man in virtue of his pursuit of the other goods, but not in virtue of his pursuit of pleasure; a man who practises aesthetic or scientific activities is thought of as admirable or commendable, but a man is not thought admirable or commendable because he enjoys himself; we have no duty to pursue our own pleasure, whereas we have a duty to pursue the other goods.

I would agree with Ross that pleasure (and absence of *pain*, in a wide sense of that word) must be a good in itself in *some* sense: the fact that someone gets pleasure from something, whether in the enjoyment or the 'being pleased' sense, must have a *prima facie* claim for consideration as a factor when other people are deciding how to act. I use this vague formula because anything more precise is controversial: there are disagreements about how to evaluate pleasure against absence of pain, how to evaluate giving people what will give them pleasure against giving them what they consciously want, how much is duty and how much goes beyond duty, and so on. I shall say a little on some of these points in chapter 4.

I would also agree with Ross that there are two different levels of goods in themselves, though his attempt to show that this is so is not without difficulties. Ross's first argument seems to me to founder for reasons I have just put forward: a so-called 'bad pleasure' could be seen as having a good element (pleasure) and a bad element (the manifestation of a cruel disposition), and the whole could then be regarded as bad without impugning the value of pleasure as such. The second argument seems to me to rest on a dubious premise: we do *not* normally call a man good for other than moral reasons, though we may of course admire and praise him for all sorts of reasons. Similarly, the third argument, based on the claim that we do not commend a man for enjoying himself, seems to me to be dubiously grounded. We certainly say things like, 'He knows how to enjoy himself', or 'He is a person who really *enjoys* life', and even, 'He is good at enjoying himself', and these seem to be commendations of some kind.

Ross might say that at least such remarks do not attribute merit or achievement, in the same way as commendations of intellectual or aesthetic or moral activity do. But this rejoinder seems neither obviously true nor obviously pertinent: not obviously true, because there may well be some deliberate effort of concentration, or exercise of imagination or self-forgetfulness, which enables a person to enjoy himself in unpromising circumstances; and not obviously pertinent, because there seems no reason to confine things good in themselves to what is within any person's deliberate grasp. For example, it might be said that a child's or simple person's unforced and untaught appreciation of some beautiful natural phenomenon is as reasonable a candidate for a good in itself as more sophisticated and critical 'aesthetic activity.'

We come then to the last of Ross's arguments: that pleasure cannot be a good in itself in the sense relevant to *eudaemonia*, because we have no duty to pursue it for ourselves as we should have if it were good in itself in the strong sense. The argument is that a true good in itself, if I may call it that, ought to be maximised for its own sake, regardless of whose life it belongs to. It makes its own claim, as it were, which is as much to be heard where it affects one's own life as where it affects anyone else's. Pleasure, it is argued, cannot be in this category, since we regard our own pleasure as having no claim on us.

This argument rests on two assumptions, neither of which have been discussed so far: that we have a duty to pursue the true good in themselves in our own lives, and that we have *no* duty to pursue pleasure for ourselves. Both these assumptions will be examined in chapter 4. Perhaps I might anticipate that discussion to explain why we do not have a duty to pursue our own happiness, as such. The importance of happiness is that it constitutes the fulfilment of the present wants of its possessor; he therefore has a right to be indifferent to it if he chooses. But one cannot have a duty which one has a right not to do. It is now clear, however, that the sense in which pleasure and happiness are goods in themselves is different from that concerned in *eudaemonia*. Bluntly, pleasure and happiness are important (objectively important) because they relate to what *is* wanted; the ingredients of *eudaemonia* are important because, whether or not they *are* wanted, they are worth wanting. The question of the relative *status* of these kinds of good – for example, the question whether we should promote the *eudaemonia* of others or their happiness – I shall discuss in chapter 4.

The thesis that pleasure is not a true good does not of course imply that there is never intrinsic worth in things done *for pleasure*. The phrase 'for pleasure' conveys two ideas. The first of these is that the activity is not part of work, is a spare-time or leisure activity. But spare-time activities are for many people the opportunity for the purest pursuit of things good in themselves. Aristotle's concept of *scholē*, or leisure, embodies this idea; for him, leisure is not a *negative* thing, freedom from work, but the positive pursuit of good activities with which work (*àscholia*, absence of leisure) interferes.[13] For Aristotle, work is for the sake of leisure.

The importance of leisure activities in *eudaemonia* must not, however, be overstated. For some people their very work (for example, as scholar or artist) is an activity good in itself, and the fact that it is also useful to them (produces their livelihood) does not detract from its value. For others their work, though basically utilitarian, can be seen as having elements of the intellectual or the aesthetic. Even Aristotle allowed that some activities good in themselves can be pursued in the course of one's business; for the soldier or statesman needs to show the moral virtues.

The second element in the meaning of the phrase 'for pleasure' concerns *motive*. If something is said to be done for pleasure, it is done, not merely as a spare-time activity, but also *with a view* to pleasure. Thus a dustman who cultivates an allotment in his spare time to eke out the family budget is not gardening *for pleasure*. Now a person may perform, for pleasure, activities which are of a type considered good in themselves: for example, listening to music. But this motive does not rob the activity of its value. On the contrary, even if these activities should turn out to be *duties*, they seem to be duties of a kind that may be better performed out of inclination than out of a sense of duty. I shall say more on this point in chapter 4.

It might be thought that at least what Aristotle called *paidiai*[14] (amusements or pastimes), that is to say, activities of which the main point is enjoyment, are now shown to have no intrinsic value. But this is too simple. Even if we take a paradigm case of *paidiai*, namely *games*, it is by no means clear that we can draw a sharp boundary between a game and a worthwhile activity. Some games can be seen as art-forms,[15] some as intellectual activities. All might on some occasion be played as an act of friendship. The most we might say here is that where an amusement seems to have no other aspect than that of producing pleasure, then it is not good in itself (in the sense previously distinguished).

I said just now that pleasure and happiness are important because they relate to what is wanted. It might now be suggested that perhaps they can be shown to be worth wanting as well, if they can be linked somehow with one of the redescriptions in terms of which I attempted to justify possible lists of goods in themselves. But I do not see how to relate pleasure or happiness to the 'distinctive human endowment' criteria. If one were seeking possible redescriptions in terms of which to attempt to justify pleasure, the ideas that come to mind are those of energy and intensity.

I have hitherto said very little about these values. They really belong to an alternative Romantic tradition, which can sometimes come into conflict with the Rationalist tradition of the human ideal, which I have so far emphasised. But the Romantic tradition is not without its links to the discussion of *eudaemonia* in the previous chapter. Thus a Romantic tradition certainly lurks in *On Liberty*, in which Mill expresses considerable admiration for strength of feeling.[16] Again, respect for this ideal, as well as for imaginative sympathy, enters into the value set on personal relationships, which are typically productive of intensities of feeling.

But appeal to an ideal of intensity cannot be used to justify a claim that *eudaemonia* entails happiness. For while the Romantic would not give the name of *eudaemonia* to a *tepid* life, his ideal would not demand that the life of *eudaemonia* should be a happy one; the Romantic ideal is equally well satisfied by pain and struggle. Indeed, the calm and tranquil kinds of happiness would not satisfy the Romantic ideal. I suggest, then, that while pleasure, if it is intense, might be thought of as valuable for Romantic reasons, a redescription in terms of intensity would not be sufficient to show that happiness is entailed by *eudaemonia*. There are of course considerable problems in any case about an intensity criterion for *eudaemonia*, at least if it is used in isolation; it seems to admit to *eudaemonia* such things as drug-induced states which we would not normally consider as possible ingredients.

A more promising approach is suggested by the idea of

self-realisation. Now if self-realisation is construed simply as fulfilling one's desires as far as possible, then it is roughly *equivalent* to happiness, as I said at the end of chapter 2, and so could not furnish a justifying redescription of it. Again, if self-realisation is the realisation of the *better* self, it cannot justify happiness as such, since precisely what is at stake is whether happiness as such is necessary for the better self. But happiness does seem to link with idiosyncratic self-realisation; not, however, in terms of the individuality which was discussed before, but in terms of *integrity* of the personality. Self-preservation, rather than self-realisation, might be the *mot juste.*

I can best explain what I mean by integrity in this context by recalling the distinction between being pleased with one's situation and acquiescence in it. The person who is merely acquiescent was depicted as in conflict and divided, always hoping for ways of getting out of his situation. Now if someone is in a position which in other respects seems to constitute *eudaemonia,* but is merely acquiescent, he is divided in this way. Suppose, for example, that a talented artist, with every opportunity to get on with his work – congenial friends, beautiful surroundings and so on – becomes discontented with this life and wants to do something less demanding: his mind and personality will be divided between the life he is leading and the life he wants to lead. If this is so, we might argue that such a life, however worthwhile its ingredients, cannot constitute *eudaemonia,* because *eudaemonia* is living a life worth living, and if a person is only *half* living it, he has not got the thing in question. Or again, if *eudaemonia* involves being a certain sort of person, a man has not got *eudaemonia* if he is divided between being one kind of person and being another.

It might therefore be possible to show along these lines that happiness is an essential part of *eudaemonia* by appeal to the idea of integrity, not in the sense that integrity offers a redescription in terms of which we can see happiness as valuable, but rather in the sense that integrity of life and personality is implied in the notion of *eudaemonia* itself. If we take this line, we can show why happiness is entailed by *eudaemonia* in a way in which pleasure in general perhaps is not; and we can show why happiness is not merely one good thing among others but of such importance that no life can be called *eudaemonia* without it.

My tentative conclusion, then, is that *eudaemonia* can be seen as a sufficient condition of hedonistic happiness, not in the empirical sense that he who has *eudaemonia* will be made happy thereby, but in the logical sense that no one can truly be said to possess *eudaemonia* unless he is happy. In this way I can connect *eudaemonia* with hedonistic happiness, but without making the two notions identical, since the possession of hedonistic happiness does not entail the possession of *eudaemonia*. We cannot say that *eudaemonia is* the best kind of hedonistic happiness, since *eudaemonia* is not in the same category at all. But we can say that it includes or embraces the best kind of hedonistic happiness.

4 Eudaemonia *as a Strategy for Hedonistic Happiness*

It might be thought that the conclusions of the previous section remove any possibility of conflict between the pursuit of *eudaemonia* and the pursuit of hedonistic happiness. But this is not the case. It is true that if a man achieves *eudaemonia* he must by definition have achieved hedonistic happiness also. But he still has the choice, if he is pursuing happiness, of whether to seek his happiness in those things which are good in themselves or whether to settle for less and look for a more mundane kind of happiness, since, as we said earlier, *eudaemonia* is not necessary for happiness.

An objector might say that this is a non-existent dilemma. It may be that in the abstract *eudaemonia* is not necessary for happiness, but in practice (the objector will say) no one can have the choice I have just mentioned. Either he will not have the conception of *eudaemonia* at all (I said earlier that there seemed to be no reason to suppose that everyone must have this conception), in which case he cannot be faced with a choice in terms of it; or he *does* possess this conception, in which case he cannot be happy with a life which does not embody it. In other words, *eudaemonia* would then be a necessary condition of *his* happiness, even if not of happiness in general. I shall consider each of these possibilities in turn.

It is true that a man who does not possess the concept of *eudaemonia* cannot see the choices he makes in terms of it. If he pursues happiness, the choices with regard to happiness will simply be whether one course of action or another is more likely to lead to it. But other people may have a problem of whether to implant the idea of *eudaemonia* into someone who seems to lack it, or whether or not to bring children up with this kind of notion. This problem is not only to do with happiness – it might be held that one ought to inculcate this conception for all kinds of reasons – but part of the problem would be: 'Granted that no policy in life can *guarantee* happiness, is a man more likely to achieve it if he forms a conception of an ideal way of life and tries to work towards that, or if he simply considers his life in terms of duties (to others) and pleasures?' In other words, the problem of whether the pursuit of *eudaemonia* is the best strategy for happiness can arise for other people, even when the person whose happiness is in question does not think in these terms.

The assertion that a man who possesses the conception of *eudaemonia* cannot be happy unless his life embodies it is an extreme overstatement of a valid idea: that the concept of *eudaemonia* must possess some 'magnetism', as Stevenson called it,[17] some implications for motivation and practice. (It might be objected that I have ruled out this possibility, by construing judgements that something is good in itself not as feelings but as beliefs as to objective facts. But I hold that a value-judgement of this kind can be construed as a particular kind of belief which necessarily carries with it a conative dimension.)[18] But the admitted magnetism of the concept of *eudaemonia* would not entail that no one who possesses this concept can be happy unless he can realise it in his life. Even if someone believed he had a *duty* to pursue *eudaemonia*, he might be able to turn his back on this duty and yet be happy – at least, this is so if I am right in my view, expressed in chapter 1, that conscience can be 'squared' sufficiently to allow happiness in defiance of duty. If, on the other hand, he sees it only as an attractive ideal, he will be drawn towards it, but not necessarily so much that he cannot be happy without it; and indeed the question would then arise whether for the sake of happiness he should endeavour to minimise in his mind the attraction of *eudaemonia*. It is only the man who is not merely attracted but emotionally committed, who has been completely and inextricably captivated by the quest for *eudaemonia*, whose happiness necessarily depends on it.

To many people, then, the question logically can present itself whether the pursuit of *eudaemonia* is the most promising strategy for pursuing happiness, whether in their own case or in someone else's. In other words: even though *eudaemonia* is not an empirically sufficient condition for happiness, is pursuing it the most likely bet nevertheless?

As the above wording suggests, this is really an empirical question rather than a philosophical one. But I can point out what the empirical points are which would need to be settled if the question is to be answered. It will be seen that many of these points refer to arguments rejected earlier, in the context of the discussions of whether *eudaemonia* is a necessary or an empirically sufficient condition for happiness. But for my present purpose weaker theses, to the effect that *eudaemonia* comes *near* to being necessary or comes *near* to being sufficient for happiness, would be just as relevant.

One question to ask in considering whether the pursuit of *eudaemonia* makes the best bet for happiness is how many people do possess some such concept *and* set great store by the idea. For *these* people happiness will not be possible without some measure of *eudaemonia*. But I would guess that they are in the minority;[19] if this is so, a claim that the pursuit of *eudaemonia* is in general the best bet for happiness cannot be based on the idea that 'for most people' a sense of their lives as constituting *eudaemonia* is essential for happiness.

A more promising avenue might be to consider that the pursuits which form the ingredients of *eudaemonia* are absorbing and extending, and so are sufficient to stave off *boredom*, a common cause of unhappiness. I said earlier that some people did not have to pursue worthwhile activities in order to avoid boredom, and I think this is true. But their avoidance of boredom did seem to depend on keeping up a good *variety* of trivia, and whether this continues to be possible depends on many contingencies. In any case, boredom is the kind of thing which suddenly strikes someone who has hitherto seemed content with trivia. So it might be the case that, for the sake of avoiding the risk of boredom, the pursuit of *eudaemonia* is a good policy for anyone.

It might be said that the suggestions of the previous paragraph do not support the view that people in search of happiness should adopt *eudaemonia*, under that description, as their aim (and, as a corollary, that they should be introduced to that concept by others if they do not possess it). What is entailed is rather that people are well advised to take an interest in one or two specific things which are supposed to have a high interest rating: for example, poetry rather than pushpin.

But this will not do. For one thing, people's aptitudes and interests vary, so it is no good fastening on some specific manifestation of a good in itself and telling people they should go for that. What people would need to do, if the anti-boredom policy is to have the best chance of success, is to find out what particular style of *eudaemonia* suits them best; and for this they need the general conception. Similarly, people's opportunities differ; it is no good their fastening on to the idea that poetry is their salvation if they cannot get hold of any.

My account so far may bring the retort that if *eudaemonia* is the best bet for happiness, many people have little chance of it. What opportunities for *eudaemonia* has a woman who works all day at an assembly line and comes home to an evening of domestic chores? Certainly, such a person has difficulties in the way of her pursuit of happiness; she does not even have *variety* in her trivial tasks. But perhaps her best chance lies in finding happiness in her friendships and personal relationships, in maintaining a lively curiosity and interest in the doings of the factory and an appreciation of any aesthetic qualities the finished products of her factory have (if she sees them!), in giving household tasks a savour by seeing them as acts of love for the family or as contributing to a beautiful home. The letters to any women's magazine illustrate the attempts some women make to do this kind of thing, and it constitutes the pursuit of a form of *eudaemonia*, even if not the richest kind.

In my earlier discussion of whether *eudaemonia* is sufficient for happiness, I stressed the *impediments* which can beset the quest for it, and which prevent it from being a guarantee of happiness. But when one is discussing whether the pursuit of *eudaemonia* is on balance the most sensible policy in the search for happiness, it is more relevant to ask whether the pursuit of *eudaemonia* is relatively less prone to impediments than the pursuit of other sources of happiness. And this has traditionally been maintained to be the case. For example, the traditional ingredients of *eudaemonia* are not so vulnerable to physical injury, illness and growing old as are physical pleasures; and not so vulnerable to the fickleness of the public as fame and success and power and popularity; and not so vulnerable as 'treasures upon earth, where moth and rust corrupt and thieves break through and steal'. The most fragile of the ingredients of *eudaemonia* is friendship, which depends on the life and on the feelings of the friends. But perhaps the kind of person who is said to have a 'gift for friendship', whose style of *eudaemonia* features friendship centrally, can find some consolation in another friend for the loss of one.

My very tentative suggestion, then, is that if the activities good in themselves are the best chance of avoiding boredom and are relatively invulnerable to misfortune, then the pursuit of such activities may offer the best chance of achieving happiness. I would stress again they do not guarantee it. As we said earlier, a person whose life is full of worthwhile ingredients may still be made unhappy by various things, including the miseries of other people.

It might be said now that this conclusion flies in the face of the popular wisdom which declares that the way to find happiness is to forget about oneself and think of other people. Now the interplay of conceptual and empirical issues that arise from this contention is exceedingly complex. I cannot hope to disentangle all the issues in this context. The most I can do here is to indicate some of the problems.

At first sight it seems that this is not an *alternative* policy to that of pursuing *eudaemonia*. Rather, it would be a special recommendation of a particular style of *eudaemonia*, one which is based on personal relationships and service to others as its chief ingredients. The champions of selflessness as the means to happiness might say that this is not what they have in mind; if a person is devoted to his family and to good causes only in order to make his *own* life a beautiful thing, then this is not 'thinking of others' at all, but a lofty kind of *self*-regard. But then it might be retorted that if he devotes his life to his family and to good causes only for the sake of his own happiness, he is also guilty of self-regard, and of a less lofty kind.

Now it is of course true that someone who is constantly reminding himself how beautiful his friendships and his community service make his life has not achieved either friendship or service, in the true sense of the terms. Nor indeed has he achieved *eudaemonia*, since the apparent goods on which he hopes to base it are spurious. In this way, too deliberate and conscious a pursuit of *eudaemonia* can be self-defeating. But it would not follow that no pursuit of *eudaemonia* is possible. A man might conceive of an ideal of *eudaemonia*, decide that for him this took the form of a life devoted to others, and then throw himself into service for others in a self-forgetful way. He might also achieve such *eudaemonia* without having originally aimed at it.

These points can be paralleled for hedonistic happiness. A person who thinks too much about how happy he will be as a result of his friendships or his service is not really going in for friendship or service. Moreover, he runs the risk of not getting the happiness in any case, since, as we saw, too self-conscious a pursuit of happiness can be self-defeating. But it is *possible* to pursue happiness through friendship and service, if a person first decides to try and do this and then, as far as day-to-day living is concerned, forgets about happiness and thinks of other people.

The parallel here between the pursuit of *eudaemonia* and the pursuit of hedonistic happiness is, however, only partial, in the following sense. The cultivation of friendships or the undertaking of service to others, if it is done too consciously for the sake of *eudaemonia*, is self-defeating for *logical* reasons: if the immediate motive for the activities is self-concerned, they are not genuine cases of friendship or of morality, and so do not bear the intrinsic value for the sake of which they are done. It is not obvious, however, that this principle must apply to all possible ingredients of *eudaemonia*. Perhaps aesthetic contemplation entails self-forgetfulness, but it is not obviously a contradiction in terms to undertake scientific research for the sake of *eudaemonia*.

When, however, it is for the sake of *happiness* that friendships or service are undertaken, this enterprise is self-defeating (if at all) for *psychological* reasons. The idea is that too much attention paid to his own attitudes prevents a person from getting absorbed in the things from which he hopes to derive his happiness. It will be recalled that I think this point is sometimes overstated, and that it is perfectly possible to plan and work for one's own happiness provided excessive self-consciousness is avoided. But what validity the point has seems equally applicable to all sources of happiness, since it concerns the psychology of pleasure, rather than the nature of its source. Indeed, one wonders whether the advice to think of other people as a means to happiness might be aptly replaced by the more general advice not to think too much about one's own reactions.

There may, however, be features of the activities of service and devotion to others which make them especially likely to make the agents in question happy. So we should now ask a partly empirical question: are those who devote their lives to others' welfare the happiest people? The accepted answer to this question is yes. But, as I have several times suggested, a potent cause of *unhappiness* for some people is the presence of misery in the world which they are powerless to alleviate. Not all those who are said to 'live for others' experience this kind of unhappiness. Perhaps it is a psychological fact that people who are succeeding in helping one person or group do not worry about other groups whom they cannot help. But in that case the advice for happiness should be not, 'Think of others', but, 'Think of those others for whom you can actually do something and take care not to get involved with anyone else'.

The other point which is relevant here, and which is not really an empirical point, is that *extreme* self-forgetfulness, so far from producing happiness, might actually be incompatible with it. When someone lives a life of saintly self-abnegation and seems to have lost all sense of self, the question whether he is pleased with his life, with its implication that there is something called 'his life' that he could contemplate, has become a meaningless one.

Perhaps, then, there are three kinds of devotion to others, or three possible stages in one life: the happy kind of devotion, which requires a sense of achievement and a feeling that one is useful, as well as concern for others; the unhappy kind, which is conscious of how little is achieved and is concerned for those who *cannot* be helped; and the self-transcendent kind, about which questions of happiness do not arise. Unless the devotee can ensure that his devotion will remain of the first kind (and he cannot, since it largely depends on factors outside his control) he will not necessarily find that concern for others is the best route to happiness.

The conclusions of this section, that the pursuit of *eudaemonia* may be the best way to pursue happiness and that devotion to others' welfare is not necessarily the best way, leave open the question of how far and in what sense people *should* pursue happiness. I turn to this question in chapter 4.

4 Happiness as the End of Life

1 *The Hypothetical Imperative to Pursue Happiness*

I turn now to the final topic of this essay: a consideration of what is meant by saying that happiness is the proper end of man, and how far it is true.

There are in fact many different ways in which the contention might be taken that happiness is the proper end of man. Traditionally the idea might be given a religious interpretation, that God's purpose for man is that he should pursue happiness. But the idea of happiness as the proper aim of man's life is appealed to in non-religious contexts, so I take it that reference to a deity is not needed to make sense of it. In any case, the idea that happiness is the proper aim of a man's life seems to make some kind of recommendation about how a man ought to conduct his life, and this cannot be *equated* with a statement about what God intends for him, though the believer might derive it from such a statement.

It may here be retorted that to speak of a 'proper' end for man need not be construed as making a recommendation at all; rather the idea is that happiness is the end which man naturally pursues by virtue of his constitution, 'proper' being construed in its sense of 'belonging'. God's intention would then be relevant after all, if it is believed that He has intentionally made man with this happiness-seeking nature. A secular version of the idea that man's nature is happiness-seeking is equally possible.

Now if this view is construed as stating that man can seek only happiness in everything he does, then not only is it not a recommendation to seek happiness but it clearly rules out the possibility of any such recommendation. As I said in chapter 1, just as we cannot be urged to seek happiness if this is impossible, so we cannot if this is necessary. The only recommendations which would be possible, and there would be plenty of point in these, would be recommendations as to the best *means* to achieve this end. But I have already argued that this view is false, and that a person does not necessarily have his own happiness as his only final goal.

It might be maintained that happiness is the proper end for man in a *third* sense: only if a man pursues happiness alone as his final goal can we really make sense of or understand his actions. I mentioned this idea briefly in chapter 1, suggesting that a belief in it and in man's essential rationality might lie behind the belief that people always act for the sake of happiness. I said there that in fact we do seem to *understand* people who sacrifice their happiness for the sake of duty, or even perhaps for the sake of some particular passion, say revenge or love. But the question might remain whether there is not *something* amiss about such conduct, whether it is not irrational in a sense which means, not that it is incomprehensible, but that it is in some way not to be recommended.

I shall assume without argument that it is not irrational to sacrifice one's own happiness for the sake of duty. This is of course a large assumption, and one that has often been challenged.[1] I cannot defend it without considering at length the whole nature of rationality. So let me simply say dogmatically that to sacrifice one's happiness for the sake of duty is to do what seems to oneself rational absolutely, in preference to what seems rational only relative to one's own preferences.

But where only one's own preferences and wishes are concerned, the question does reasonably arise whether there is not a sense in which one *ought* to seek happiness, and indeed ought to subordinate other things to it. The 'ought' here seems to be that of the Kantian hypothetical or prudential imperative, based on a man's wants. Whereas the moral imperative is, 'You should', the prudential imperative is, 'Given that you want, you should.' For if we ask why someone ought to seek his own happiness, it might seem natural to reply 'in his own interest', or 'for his own sake'. And this is to say, employing Kantian terminology, 'in obedience to the hypothetical imperative'.

Now it should be noted that to say that someone ought to

seek happiness is not the same as saying that he ought, for happiness's sake, to do something else. I suggested in chapter 3 that the most likely way of achieving happiness might be to pursue *eudaemonia*. This conclusion might be expressed in the form of the hypothetical imperative, 'You ought to seek *eudaemonia*', where what is implied is that *eudaemonia* is the best means to happiness, and happiness as an end is presupposed. But the question at issue now is whether it makes sense to say, in the same sense, that people *ought* to seek happiness itself. There are grave difficulties in such a notion. Firstly, the idea of a prudential *imperative* is in any case not a very clear one. Secondly, in so far as it *can* be made sense of, it would normally concern means rather than ends. Thirdly, and most fundamentally, the idea of telling someone to seek *happiness itself* for prudential reasons seems somehow trivial and indeed tautologous (if an imperative can be said to be tautologous). I shall say something on each of these difficulties in turn.

One sometimes comes across the idea that the prudential *imperative* is a confused notion. According to this idea, the only true imperative (in Kant's sense of 'imperative') is the categorical or moral imperative. Only in this sense can one say that a person *ought* to do something, and the so-called prudential imperative is simply a combination of two factual propositions, that a certain thing is wanted and that certain means are efficacious for obtaining it.

But whatever the prudential imperative means, we cannot reduce it in this way to the reasoning which supports it. People who utter prudential imperatives are not stating facts about wants and means, but using considerations of wants and means as reasons for *justifying* actions to their friends: they say, 'You want X; Y is a means to X; *so* you ought . . .', and so on. In other words, the reasoning here is not a mere theoretical syllogism, yielding the theoretical conclusion, 'so Y is a means to what you want'. It has a bearing on action analogous to that of a moral judgement, such that something needs explaining if a man accepts the premises of the prudential imperative and then does not act accordingly. The nature of this imperative is obscure, just as is the nature of the moral imperative, but this does not mean that it can be eliminated.

The second problem is that a hypothetical imperative concerns means to an end the desire for which is presupposed, whereas an imperative to pursue happiness seems to be the prescription of an *end*. The prescription of an end is a doubly difficult idea. Firstly, the bindingness, such as it is, which inheres in the hypothetical imperative seems to rest on the practical link between desiring an end and desiring the means to it. Secondly, we cannot desire things at will, so it would seem that we cannot be told to adopt an end.

These difficulties can be met, however, if we take the imperative to pursue happiness, not as an imperative to *desire* an end, but as an imperative to *pursue* one. Such an imperative presupposes desire for the end, and is saying in effect 'Don't just desire, *do* something', or, more formally, 'Since you desire such-and-such, you ought to take whatever means are available to secure it.' Now we certainly sometimes say to people and, more relevantly, they say to themselves that since they want a certain thing they ought to 'do something' (unspecified, but whatever is effective) about getting it. The 'ought' of this kind of imperative rests on the connection between desiring an end and desiring the means to it, just as does that of the more informative kind of hypothetical imperative; and although it may be couched in the form, 'Pursue X', where X is the end, what is being prescribed is the adoption of means. I suggest that the hypothetical imperative, 'You ought to pursue happiness', would make sense if construed in this way, as what we may call an 'uninformative' hypothetical imperative; it would mean, in effect, 'Since you desire happiness, you ought to do whatever you can about getting it.'

Nor do I think this happiness-hypothetical would be a mere tautology. It is not saying, 'It is conducive to happiness to pursue happiness', or indeed making any statement at all; but rather appealing to the reasonableness of pursuing what you want, a thing which people do not always do.

But if we are to hold that it is in this sense that happiness is the proper end for *everyone*, it must be shown that everyone does possess the desire for happiness on which this imperative rests. I have however argued that this is not so, and that not everyone desires happiness. If I am right in this, it follows that happiness is not the proper end of *everyone*, in the sense under discussion. The most one could say is that there are those who do want happiness as such, and to whom the 'uninformative' hypothetical imperative *can* be addressed, 'Since you want happiness, you ought to do something about it.' This is an exemplification of Kant's principle that, 'He· who wills the end wills the means',[2] (*qua* rational agent, one must assume) with the end specified, but with the means left unspecified.

But this imperative is really concerned, not with happiness in particular, but with anything that is wanted but not sought. It addresses itself to the person who wants happiness but does nothing about it, but it gives no *special* pre-eminence to happiness, and so it has nothing to say to the person who normally pursues happiness but is threatening to throw it all away for the sake of some 'particular passion': for example, the person who intends to marry someone with whom he knows he will not be happy, and without whom he knows he can soon be happy again. To such a person, an injunction to pursue happiness cannot mean simply, 'Try to get what you want', since he is equally doing that if he sets about marrying the unsuitable spouse. It must mean, 'Do the most reasonable thing', on the assumption that it is somehow more reasonable to pursue happiness than to pursue a particular passion, where these conflict.

Now it is often perfectly *comprehensible* that someone should sacrifice his happiness for a particular passion. Indeed in the kind of case I have mentioned it seems more than usually comprehensible that someone should decide against happiness. In saying this I am not thinking primarily of the possibility that the person may think he has incurred a moral obligation in the matter; as I said earlier, explanation is not called for if one prefers duty to happiness. Nor am I thinking of the likelihood that the reason why the person in question sacrifices his happiness is sheer *cowardice*, which is explicable enough. Nor do I have in mind the fact that in this kind of case people typically have rather *ambivalent* views as to where their future happiness is likely to lie: 'Life with the beloved will be stormy but at least it will never be *dull*, life without the beloved would be tranquil but perhaps it would be very boring', and so on.

Any of these considerations would make sense of a decision against happiness. But an especially pertinent consideration, in this kind of case, is the thought people sometimes have that one can be *too* rational, too calculating. To say to a person who feels like this that he ought to pursue happiness because it would be more rational is in fact *counter*-productive; he feels that there can come a time when passion is to be preferred to reason. This idea is to be distinguished from the belief that the best way to achieve happiness may be to stop trying to get it; the thought is not that one can be too rational to achieve happiness but that one can be too rational altogether. This is a manifestation of the Romantic ideal which I touched on briefly earlier – or rather of the Romantic temperament, since a person may decide against his happiness without seeing himself as pursuing any specific ideal. With such a person the idea of choosing happiness because it is the rational choice will cut no ice.[3]

In the face of these considerations, it is worth trying to look more closely at why the pursuit of happiness *is* to be regarded as more rational than the pursuit of an individual passion. First of all compare the happy life with the life which lacks happiness. It will be recalled that the happy life is one with which its owner is pleased: he wants to hang on to it, not in the sense of mere acquiescence, but wholeheartedly and without conflict. A life which lacks happiness is one to which its owner is indifferent, or which he strives actively to change, or which, while having decided to acquiesce in it, he regards with divided feelings. It is clear, then, that a happy life by definition meets one's wants (at the time of living it) more than a life which lacks happiness. And if wants are the basis of reasons for action, as far as oneself is concerned, then a happy life is a more reasonable choice than a life which lacks happiness.

But the recognition that this *would* be the reasonable choice is often not operative in practice. Quite apart from the point I have made about the Romantic temperament, which deliberately eschews what is reasonable, there is the fact that the relative strength of a person's feelings at one time does not necessarily correspond with the relative extent to which his wants will be realised at a later time. He can feel strongly about some particular end and be indifferent to his future happiness, although the future happiness represents a much greater satisfaction of wants. (Not necessarily the *same* wants as before: happiness means having what you want now, or wanting what you have now, rather than having what you wanted before.)

This is why an imperative enjoining the pursuit of happiness is not otiose; it says, in effect, '*Given* that the point of doing anything is to fulfil your wants, then the most pointful thing to do is to pursue happiness.' But it is up against the psychological barrier that pursuing happiness can seem positively *irrational* at the time, since it can mean ignoring a clamorous want and acting in a way which, as it were, 'feels' unmotivated.

It will be seen that this account of the rational claims of happiness rests on a person's eventually being pleased with the life which produces happiness, rather than on his wanting happiness as such. Can we therefore regard the imperative to pursue happiness as binding even on those who do not want it at all? One of the difficulties about a hypothetical imperative concerning happiness was said to be that we cannot adopt ends at will. But now it seems that this consideration is not really relevant. A person does not have to want happiness in order to be a suitable recipient of the imperative, 'You ought to pursue happiness', since it rests its credentials on what the happy person will want to hang on to when he is happy, rather than on what he wants now before he is happy. Moreover, the assumption is often made, as when one says, 'Think of your future happiness', to someone who is about to marry the wrong person, that people *can* act against their present inclinations, for the sake of future satisfactions which do not at present seem important. If this is a valid assumption, there seems no difficulty in saying, 'You ought to pursue happiness', to those who at present have no desire for it as such at all. The point of saying it would be, in effect, 'You want some things and you think it reasonable to act to get them. How much more reasonable to aim at achieving a state in which you have everything you want, the life which you would not want to change.'

If these lines of argument are sound, we can show happiness to be an appropriate or proper end for everyone, in the following sense: there is a kind of hypothetical imperative to the effect that, given that the satisfaction of wants is the general reason for acting, the most reasonable policy is to aim at a situation which constitutes general satisfaction of wants. Note that the imperative does not concern the best means of satisfying specific present wants. Happiness may depend on a man's ignoring his present wants. Rather it is addressed to man as a wanting animal in general: 'Since you are a wanter, you should aim at the state of having what you want (or wanting what you have) in all respects.' This is not, of course, a *Kantian* hypothetical in form, since it does not prescribe means to a desired end. Nor does it possess quite the necessity inherent in 'He who wills the end, wills the means.' But it addresses itself to the rationality of want-satisfaction, and I call it a hypothetical imperative for this reason.

2   Happiness and Moral Duty

The 'ought' or 'should' of the hypothetical imperative is not, of course, the only kind of 'ought' or 'should'. Another obvious sense in which it can be said that a person *should* do something is the moral sense; so I think it is worth considering now whether we can be said to have a moral duty to seek happiness – our own happiness, that is.

There is of course a theory of ethics according to which this is our *only* duty. I do not wish to spend any time discussing ethical egoism, as it seems to me too implausible, at least if it is regarded as an account of our normal 'moral convictions', 'moral intuitions', and the like. But there are various possible arguments for the thesis that we have *a* duty (one among others) to seek our own happiness. I intend to spend a little time discussing these, although I would allow that to say merely that *one* of our duties is to seek our own happiness would be a weak account of the thesis that happiness is *the* proper end for man.

I have said that there are various possible arguments for the view that we have a duty to seek our own happiness. This may seem surprising, especially if I emphasise that I mean 'seek it for its own sake', and not 'seek it as means': for example, as a hedge against temptation, as Kant recommends. [4] So I must first try to dismiss the considerations which might seem to rule out such a duty as even a possible idea. For example, it is sometimes said that we cannot have any duties which are not duties to other people. Now it is true that the *word* 'duty' is most often used in the plural, in the context of a contractual or quasi-contractual situation. But the *idea* of a duty need not be confined to such situations, unless it is thought that all morality is grounded in undertakings; and we can speak of 'what we ultimately ought to do' if the connotations of the word 'duty' are too awkward. Similarly, it may be alleged that morality is by definition concerned with the reconciliation of conflicting *interests*, and so cannot concern one person alone. If this is merely a stipulation about how the word 'morality' is to be used, I have no objection to it, since I could talk instead about 'ultimate oughts' or 'the content of the categorical imperative'. But it surely cannot be true by definition that there are no 'ultimate oughts' other than those which concern inter-personal relationships. This is a substantive thesis, and to assume it would be not to refute but only to beg the question against the hypothesis I wish to examine.

A more fundamental attempt to undercut the thesis in question from the start appeals to the idea that morality (or 'ultimate oughts' if you like) is at least to be contrasted with *inclination*. On this view, the whole point of saying that a person morally ought to do something is that the something is an action which he might not otherwise be inclined to do; so it is odd to speak of a duty to seek happiness.

This objection can however be met by reminding ourselves again that not everyone actually always does what is conducive to his happiness, so there would after all be some point in telling us to seek it. It is perhaps true that we must *have an interest* in our own happiness, in a sense in which we do not necessarily have an interest in anything else. But since having this interest does not necessarily produce motivation, it would not render otiose the putative moral injunction to seek happiness.

The first argument I shall consider in favour of the duty of happiness, as I shall call the thesis for short, is that drawn from the existence of a certain kind of *shame*. Sometimes, when people do not manage to be happy, they feel shame and self-disgust: 'How is it that I cannot manage to be happy given all my many advantages in life?' – and so on. It might be objected that there are many kinds of shame, and not all kinds are shame at a failure in *duty*: I can be ashamed of my stammer, my fat legs, etc., although I would never think I had a duty not to stammer or to have thin legs. This objection is inadequate as it stands, since it might be said that people who are ashamed of not being *happy* recognize that their failure to be happy is due to a fault which is usually thought of as a *moral* fault: self-centredness, cowardice, lack of tenacity or patience, intemperance and so on. But to point this out does not save the argument, since actions exemplifying even these faults need not be failures to do one's duty. Character-traits are sometimes thought of as virtues or vices because they exemplify the presence or absence of forms of *self-mastery*, whether the self-mastery or its lack is shown in a moral context or not.

A more substantial argument for the duty of happiness is a kind of universalisability argument in reverse. It might be argued that on any view of morality we are thought to have some obligation to respect, or even to foster, the happiness of others. If this is so, it must be because their happiness is morally important – and in that case, surely our own must be equally important, make an equal moral claim?

The first step in meeting this argument is to challenge the premise, that we have duties in respect of others' happiness. I would suggest that our duty is rather in respect of their *ends*; thus it would be impertinent to do things for people which they did not want, even if we believed (however plausibly) that we would thereby make them happy. But if the universalisability-in-reverse argument is sound this would mean that we have a duty to pursue our own ends, which does not make sense. I think the solution is to reject the reverse universalisability argument itself, as based on the false assumption that our own position and that of others are symmetrical in morality. On the contrary, it might well be said, part of the idea of morality is *asymmetrical* in essence: namely, that we should extend to others the interest we naturally have in ourselves and treat others' ends as our own.[5]

The third argument for the duty to pursue our own happiness which I wish to consider appeals to the fact that we do not consider ourselves to be obliged always to sacrifice our own happiness to that of others. What I mean here is that without guilt we spend on our own pursuits large amounts of money and time which could transform the lives of those in need if spent on them instead. I am not necessarily thinking of donations to Oxfam, or the like. I am supposing that for example we could make many lonely old or sick people who do not expect much of life happy, if we spent our spare time visiting them; that we might make ourselves less happy if we spent all our free time in this way; and that we do not think ourselves obliged to sacrifice our happiness in this way (though we may consider ourselves obliged to do something).

This 'phenomenon of the moral consciousness' can be used as follows in an argument for the duty to pursue happiness. On any common view of morality we have a duty, whether or not it is seen as the only duty, to promote others' happiness, or rather as I have said their ends. If then we think we are sometimes justified in ignoring others' happiness for the sake of our own, this could only be (so the argument goes) because we have a more 'stringent' obligation with respect to our own: for only a duty can morally outweigh a duty.

Now one way to rebut this argument is to take the heroic step of declaring that we are all simply *complacent*, and that we *should* be feeling guilty at our neglect of others and our failure to sacrifice our happiness. But I think that without taking such a drastic step we can still avoid drawing the conclusion that we have a duty towards our own happiness. One way of doing this would be to say that we *do* have a duty to ourselves, but it is not a duty to foster our own happiness as such. Our duty to ourselves is rather to cultivate our talents, develop our intellects, and so on; and it is in pursuit of *this* aim that we are sometimes (not always) justified in placing ourselves before others. The trouble with this defence, however, is that it is too 'highbrow'. I do not wish to deny the possibility of such duties to ourselves: on the contrary, as will be seen in the next section. But I would find it difficult to maintain that we are justified in placing ourselves first only in those situations where our self-development, rather than our happiness as such, is at stake.

A second way of meeting this argument is to say that the scope of others' moral claims on us is a much more limited one than such formulae as, 'Make others' ends your own', or, 'Promote the greatest happiness of the greatest number', would suggest. Thus, for example, it might be said that all we are morally bound to do, special obligations apart, is to refrain from causing misery and from preventing happiness; we need not take steps actually to relieve misery or to promote happiness. We might call this view passive utilitarianism, and it reflects many people's moral practice. But there is then a real question whether the distinction between action and omission can carry as much moral weight as this system requires: why should it be wrong to *cause* misery, but permissible not to relieve it when you can?

The third possibility is to invoke the idea of a limited moral *right* to pursue happiness. It is usually assumed that we possess a minimum right of *recipience* to pursue happiness: the right that others should at least not frustrate our efforts or cause us misery.[6] But I think this right of recipience implies that there is no wholesale duty on our part to subordinate our happiness entirely to that of others; in other words, it implies also a right of *action*. For it would be pointless to say to A that he must refrain from some pet project in order to respect B's right to happiness, and at the same time say to B that he has a duty to give up his happiness altogether if he can please A by doing so. I conclude that it must be morally permissible to pursue our own happiness to some degree, and that there is therefore no need to invoke a *duty* to pursue happiness in order to explain the moral room for manoeuvre that we seem to have.

The fourth attempt to argue that we have a duty to pursue our own happiness is based on an assertion that it is a good thing for people to be happy; happiness as such is valuable in itself. If this is so, the argument continues, surely it should be fostered wherever possible, whether in one's own case or another's.

Now one reply which may at first suggest itself, namely that happiness is of subjective value only, is based on an error, as we saw in chapter 3. But all the same the kind of objective value that happiness has is such that it does not give rise to duties for the person whose happiness it is, whatever might be said about duties to others in respect of it. For presumably what is good about people's being happy is that happiness is a state of wants fulfilled. But if the person whose wants are in question is not concerned about whether they are fulfilled or not, there does not seem to be any point of view from which to insist that nevertheless he morally ought to pursue happiness. No one else is involved and the value of the happiness rests solely on the interest of the man concerned; so any putative 'duty' could be waived by him at will.

It will be seen that this argument is a kind of complement to that mentioned at the beginning of the section. There I said that, since interest does not necessarily breed inclination, a man is not necessarily motivated to pursue his own interests, and so the idea of a duty to pursue one's own happiness cannot be ruled out on the ground that there is a necessary inclination to do so which makes meaningless the ascription of duty. The present argument is that a man's own interest, as such, may be said to be his own affair: if *he* is not interested in his interest, there is no other person or value in the name of which a duty can be prescribed to him.

It might now be suggested that happiness might *also* have another kind of objective value, one which depends on values other than simply its being in the interest of its possessor. I considered in chapter 3 some possibilities of showing this. I suggested there that Romantic qualities of energy and intensity might describe the more ecstatic forms of happiness, but they would not apply to the more tranquil kinds and were also perhaps rather doubtful as unqualified descriptions of something good. But I also considered happiness as a manifestation of *integrity* of the personality, and by this means made happiness by definition part of *eudaemonia*, on the grounds that happiness is necessary for an integrated life, and integratedness of life is part of the definition of *eudaemonia*. I should like now to look at this notion of integrity again, and consider whether a case can be made out for saying that we have a moral duty to pursue our own happiness, not regarded as such, but regarded as an essential part of our personal integrity. If the best way of pursuing happiness is by pursuing *eudaemonia*, as I suggested earlier, then this hypothesis will generate at one remove a hypothesis that we have a duty to pursue *eudaemonia* as a means to happiness. But for the moment my concern is not with *eudaemonia*, but with hedonistic happiness from whatever source.

Now 'integrity', needless to say, can mean a great many things, and the senses most naturally connected with duty do not seem to be those most naturally connected with happiness. Thus a person of integrity may be one who is scrupulously honest, just and incorruptible; clearly we have a duty to try to have *this* kind of integrity, but this integrity has no particular connection with happiness. Again, a person of integrity may be one who is more than usually loyal to his convictions; this is the essence of duty, or at least of dutifulness, but hardly of happiness.

We get nearer to happiness with a third sense of 'integrity', that which is roughly equivalent to *sincerity*; a man of integrity in this sense is one who does not say one thing to one person and another to another, or pretend to agree when he does not. (It is of course a matter for discussion just how far we have a duty to be like this.) This kind of integrity is still not the *same* as that involved in happiness, but it approaches it, involving as it does some idea of a person who is the same through and through. The happiness sense of 'integrity' is one for which perhaps the word 'integratedness' might more idiomatically be used; the happy person is one whose life and personality are well integrated and free from conflict. Unlike integrity of the other three kinds, this kind of integrity does not have an obvious moral dimension. But I think we can nevertheless see it as giving rise to a duty if we connect it with the notion of *respect for persons*.

This Kantian idea, when 'cashed out' in terms of principles for action, is partly a matter of treating others' *ends* as one's own: an idea which, as we saw earlier, gives rise to no duties to oneself. But it is also concerned with values which are not concerned with ends at all: with the importance of each individual as a separate and unique centre of consciousness and choice. It might be retorted that Kant himself, so far from valuing the individual, is apt to suggest that individual human beings are valuable only as embodying an abstract quality of personhood. Be that as it may, the modern version of the Kantian principle, usually expressed as respect for the individual, lays as much stress on individuality as on personhood as such. Anyone who makes respect for the individual his guiding moral principle will be committed thereby to regarding *himself* as one of these valuable individuals who ought to be cherished, quite independently of his own wants in the matter.

In the light of these considerations, we can see why the integratedness of happiness might be regarded as something a person has a duty to achieve if he can. A person who is integrated in this way displays to a special degree that unity which makes a man *a person*, an individual character, as distinct from a bundle of unconnected emotions. The happy person *is* wholeheartedly one particular sort of person, rather than one person in fact and another in wish. Anyone who feels that he ought to respect human personality, in himself and in others, might reasonably feel that among his duties is that of so ordering himself and his life that a harmonious whole is the result.

Two lines of objection to this train of thought suggest themselves. The first is that these considerations, though they might demonstrate that happiness is to be aimed at in so far as it represents integratedness, are of a kind to suggest *ideals*, rather than duties; perhaps on the grounds that one cannot have any duty concerning oneself, or because the claims of integratedness are not important or stringent enough. I shall discuss this kind of contention at length in the next section, so I will not stop to deal with it here. The second line of objection is the obvious one, that there must be times when one ought not to pursue happiness and kinds of happiness one ought to pursue. Indeed, it may be integrity itself of the more strictly moral kind which demands a sacrifice of integratedness. But this is quite consistent with the thesis that the pursuit of happiness is a duty. For I would not wish to maintain that it is more than a *prima facie* duty, which can be overridden on some occasions.

I conclude then – and once more this is a rather tentative conclusion – that people have not merely a moral right to pursue their own happiness, but also a duty to do so. But this duty is not concerning happiness as embodying one's own interest, but rather concerning happiness as embodying the integratedness of the personality of the individual concerned.

But if the principle of respect for persons is accepted as a basic moral principle, there is also another ground on which one might argue that we have a *prima facie* duty to pursue our own happiness. We saw in the previous section that the pursuit of happiness was more *rational* than the unsystematised pursuit of different ends or the sacrifice of happiness for the sake of one of them. But rationality is the essence of personhood. It might be argued, then, that a person who is trying to respect person-hood in himself has a duty to pursue happiness, not because happiness is the state in which his wants are fulfilled (this fact grounds a merely hypothetical obligation), but because the pursuit of happiness, rather than the enslavement to caprice or drifting along without an overall plan, is what befits a *person*.

As before, this duty to be happy because happiness is rational is a *prima facie* duty. It may well be the case that it sometimes comes into conflict, either with our duty to treat others' ends as our own, or with the duty to pursue *eudaemonia* which I shall expound in the next section. The first type of conflict must I think be weighted in favour of the ends of others, since the rationality involved in treating others' ends as one's own is, as it were, a higher *brand* of rationality, rationality absolute as distinct from rationality as applied to one's own concerns. It might be thought that the second type of conflict cannot arise, if *eudaemonia* by definition includes happiness and if the pursuit of *eudaemonia* is in general the most likely way of securing happiness. But a person might be so exceptionally placed that his chances of achieving *eudaemonia*, and happiness in it, are slight and his best chance of happiness is to try to teach himself to be pleased with an impoverished and subhuman type of life. This is clearly the rational thing to do from the point of view of his own interests, and so he is subject to a *hypothetical* imperative that he ought to learn to like his impoverished life. But I think respect for persons probably demands that he keep alive a love of the kind of life that really befits a person, even at the cost of some degree of happiness if he cannot attain it.

This discussion of a possible duty to pursue happiness has been concerned with happiness as such, happiness from any source. If it is thought that this kind of duty is too far-fetched, we can point out that for many people the same actions that would be involved in the pursuit of happiness might in any case be regarded as duties for another reason. For I have suggested that in general the best way to pursue happiness may be through a pursuit of *eudaemonia*; and I now wish to argue for a duty to pursue *eudaemonia* as such.

3. *The Duty to Pursue* Eudaemonia

It might at first seem as though it must be *analytic* that we have a duty to pursue *eudaemonia*. *Eudaemonia* was *defined* as the life worth wanting, fit to be pursued, and so on. Moreover, I was at pains to stress that the sense of 'worth', 'fit', and so on, was not to be understood in merely prudential and contingent terms, dependent ultimately on people's actual wants, but rather on an 'objective' valuation. What can this mean (it might be said) except that we have a duty or obligation to pursue *eudaemonia*?

I do not wish to deny that this conception of the good in itself does not make sense unless it carries some implications about what people *ought* (in a non-hypothetical sense) to do. But we cannot translate every statement of the form, 'This is good in itself', into a statement of the form, 'I have a moral duty to pursue this'. For one thing, there might well be things good in themselves which are not very obviously pursuable, such as states of mind, feelings, and so on: compassion for others' sufferings and joy at some beautiful sight might be possible examples. Here the goodness in itself seems to amount to a claim that such things are rightly *valued*. For another thing, the claim that something is good in itself, even where it does allow of action, does not seem to entail that I should pursue the good for *myself*. If, for example, intellectual activity is held to be a good in itself, this presumably entails that it should *be fostered* as far as possible. But whether any one person should foster it by undertaking it himself or by encouraging others to do so remains an open question.

I suggest that if the notion of the good in itself, as I have expounded it so far, is a coherent one, it must entail the moral fittingness of a *group* of responses in human beings, their exact nature varying with the case: thus some goods in themselves will be fittingly wanted and valued and cherished, others will be fittingly fostered and promoted as well. In the latter case duties are directly involved, in the former case only indirectly, if at all (perhaps, for example, duties to foster certain attitudes in children might be entailed). This notion of 'fittingness' thus straddles the voluntary and involuntary; I see nothing particularly controversial in this, as we often want to say in quite ordinary situations both that one ought morally to feel a certain way and that one ought to do certain things, while recognising that the latter 'oughts' are under one's control in a way that the former are not. I suggest further that, if the responses are in respect of that which is said to be good in itself, they must be indifferent as to who will possess the good in question. The most fitting response, as far as the good in itself is concerned, will be that which promotes *it* most effectively, and this might involve either doing something oneself or encouraging or enabling others to do so.

Here, however, I encounter a difficulty. It will be recalled that I suggest at the end of chapter 2 that *eudaemonia* might be regarded as something to which an individual had a right and in the pursuit of which he might sometimes come in conflict with others. I have also suggested that *eudaemonia* might be regarded as constituting each man's good or welfare, in that sense of the words 'good', 'welfare', which does not depend on the individual's wants. It seems then that the promotion of *eudaemonia* cannot after all be indifferent as between one person's exhibiting it and another. The distribution of *eudaemonia* will be important as well as its maximisation, if each individual has a right to it.

It seems that we really have two different ideas at work here. One stresses abstract 'values', the other human perfection. One stresses goods in themselves as having a life of their own, as it were; the other, their immersion in a whole – *eudaemonia* – which constitutes an individual's welfare. Both conceptions, of course, are realised only in specific human lives. But there can on occasion be a tension between them: for example, should resources be spent on supporting a few geniuses in an abstruse field in mathematics who will 'advance the subject', or on making a whole group of children a little more numerate? Fortunately such possible conflicts are rare. For often it will come about that to promote the good activity of one individual – say, a musician – in a way which may seen inequitable is in fact to foster the *eudaemonia* of many others – here in respect of their opportunity to listen to music – at one remove. In practice, then, the same action in this sphere could often be regarded either as fulfilling a duty to maximise the good in itself or as fulfilling a duty to make the lives of human beings, including ourselves, as rich as possible in what is worth having. In any case, there are people who would regard as meaningless all talk of goods in themselves as having any kind of value other than their contribution to individuals' well-being: thus to them 'service to mathematics' or 'service to music', as in a citation for a knighthood, must mean, not service to these things in the abstract, but 'service to the mathematical or musical life of *people*, of the community'.

In what follows, I shall concentrate on the ingredients of *eudaemonia* as constituting the good of individuals, and I shall argue for the view that we have a duty to promote this good both in our own case and in that of others; in this section I shall argue for the duty to ourselves, and in the next for that to others.

As an illustration of the kind of situation where it is natural to speak of a duty to promote one's own *eudaemonia*, consider the following kind of case. A neurotic and tyrannical widow keeps an only daughter at home to look after her. The girl is intelligent and talented and not without charm, but she does nothing all day except fetch and carry for the mother, who wrongly fancies herself an invalid. The daughter's attempts to form friendships are frustrated by the mother's jealousy and carping criticism, and her attempts to read anything demanding or cultivate talents are sneered out of existence. The mother is emotionally very dependent on her daughter and will be wretched if she leaves home.

I suggest that most people, while allowing that daughters have a *prima facie* duty to look after widowed mothers and that we all have a *prima facie* duty to avoid causing suffering to others, would say that the daughter ought to leave home. And this is not merely the view that she ought for *prudential* reasons to do so. Indeed, she may be becoming perfectly happy at home, and if so this will seem to onlookers not the least distressing aspect of the situation. Nor is the verdict merely that she has a moral *right* to leave home. A right may be waived, and this daughter, out of cowardice or apathy or a mistaken sense of duty, might well waive her right. I should hold that a common view would be that she has a *duty* to leave home, perhaps expressed in such terms as that she owes it to herself to do so. If backing for this verdict were sought, it would be in such terms as these: 'As she is, she's scarcely a person in her own right at all – she's got a lot of potential that she ought to develop – it's wicked to waste oneself – we've all got capacities and we ought to use them', and so on. These views are articulations of an idea of respect for personhood, or for the characteristic human endowment, as something which everyone should strive to show towards himself.

But there is also opposition to the idea of duties to oneself. As I said earlier, when discussing the duty to pursue happiness, it is sometimes maintained that morality by definition concerns others. If this is just a question of how the *word* 'moral' is usually used, I am quite content to say that this kind of duty to oneself is not a *moral* duty, provided I can still maintain that it is a categorical obligation in the Kantian sense and that it may on occasion (as in my example) outweigh *prima facie* moral duties. But it is sometimes argued that the idea of a categorical obligation to oneself does not make sense. For example, a reader of Mill might combine his doctrine that people have no right to compel others to act in a certain way in spheres where only the agent is affected[7] with his doctrine that a duty is something which others may exact,[8] and so come to the conclusion that there can be no duty to oneself.

The way out of this particular argument is to deny the second thesis, which Mill in any case did not consistently hold. It may be that duties *to specific people* can rightly be exacted by those people, but even in the sphere of duties to others it seems implausible to talk of a right of exactment in some cases: for example, the duty to subscribe to charity. It would be more plausible to say that duty is something neglect of which always incurs *blame* from others. But then failure in what I have called duties to oneself *does* incur blame from onlookers, if they think that the person whose duty is in question is capable of acting and does not do so.

A second point of view from which it might be argued that one cannot have a duty to pursue one's own *eudaemonia* is provided by the idea that *eudaemonia* embodies one's *interest*, in one sense of that word, and one cannot have a duty to pursue one's own interest. Now it is true that *eudaemonia* represents a person's 'true interest', 'what it would be best for him to be and have', and so on. But the reasons which might be held to preclude the possibility of having a duty to pursue one's own interest do not apply to this kind of interest. One of these reasons concerns *motive*: duty, it is said, must be something which we may not have an inclination to do. But *eudaemonia*, which is not defined in terms of its possessor's wants at all, has no necessary connection with inclination. (Indeed, interest in the *prudential* sense does not seem to have either, as we have seen.) The second reason concerns the alleged right to waive any consideration dependent only on one's own interest: this, it may be said, undermines from the start any talk of duty to pursue one's own interest. But belief in such a right would rest on the view that, if the importance of one's interests depends ultimately only on one's wants, one can, as it were, cancel out that importance by not *wanting* to be bothered. If the interest in question is of a different kind, not to be cashed out in terms of wants, then the alleged right to waive consideration of it has no foundation.

A connected argument against the idea that we have a duty to pursue our own *eudaemonia* rests on the idea that duties and rights are *correlative*: if A has a duty to B, B has a right against A. But if this is so (the argument goes on) we cannot have a duty to ourselves. For if we did, we should have a right against ourselves; and since one can always waive a right, one can always dissolve the alleged duty at will.

One way out of this argument would be to say that the duty in question is not really to *ourselves*, but to personhood or ultimate good or something of the kind, and we simply happen to be the 'location' of the duty. But whether or not one believes in the intelligibility of duties to or concerning such an abstraction, I think we should be reluctant to let go of the other idea, that each person as an individual, including ourselves, has some right to *eudaemonia*. If we hold on to the latter notion, even alongside the 'abstract values' notion, we still have the difficulty.

A better way out of the difficulty is to challenge the assumption that all rights can be waived. This does not seem to be obviously the case, even with rights against others. Take the common doctrine that everyone has a right to liberty, or in other words that everyone has a duty not to enslave others. Suppose someone says, 'I waive my right to liberty; you may enslave me', does that make it permissible to do so? Surely not, since the right to liberty does not rest only on the rebuttable presumption that everyone wants liberty, but also on a value that attaches to liberty independently of the desires of its possessor. In the same way, the right to *eudaemonia* is not to be waived, since its value does not rest on its possessor's desires, and so the duty to pursue it is not dissoluble.

Of course the idea of rights against oneself is a *metaphor*, just as is the idea of duties to oneself; the two roles the person sustains, as agent and as beneficiary, are treated as though they constituted two separate people. But there is nothing in the fact that this is a metaphor to render incoherent the idea of duties of the kind I have been discussing.

It might now be admitted that there are duties to oneself of the kind under discussion, but suggested that they are some-how less *important* than duties to others. For example, it might be thought that duties to others always take precedence. But this does not seem always to be the case in our ordinary thinking, as my example of the put-upon daughter shows. Alternatively, it might be thought that the so-called duties to self arise for an individual only if he has decided to espouse some *ideal* which is not itself obligatory. Now it is true that there might be room for an individual to choose in what *way* to realise his *eudaemonia*. But if general ideas of a life good in itself and of the distinctive endowment of a person make any moral claim, then it is one to which all moral agents *qua* persons are subject, whether or not they acknowledge the claim.

An objector might fasten on the word 'ideal' in the above, and say that, even if the claim of *eudaemonia* is not that of an ideal in the sense of being self-selected or self-imposed, it certainly is in the sense of going beyond the minimum required for morali-ty, that which the agent is to be blamed for omitting. Now I do not necessarily wish to dissolve the distinction between duties and supererogatory acts,[9] but this distinction does not coincide with that between duties to others and alleged duties to self. As we saw earlier, it seems possible to *blame* someone for failure in duty to himself, and if this is so, then duty to oneself can sometimes be a true duty in the 'minimum requirement' sense. Of course there will be less likelihood of others' *expressing* blame where only the agent himself is affected. For one thing, they will not have the same practical interest in doing so. For another, it will not always be obvious to an onlooker whether the agent concerned is not pursuing *eudaemonia* at all or simply selecting a narrow and specialised interpretation of it, whereas many duties to others (though not all) are exceedingly cut and dried and admit of no uncertainty as to whether a breach has taken place.

I have implicitly left open the possibility that in the sphere of morality concerning oneself there may be both duties (minimum requirements) and actions which go beyond duty. I do not want to try to draw a line between these two, particularly as the distinction itself is perhaps problematic (is it not perhaps blameworthy to some extent to lead a less good life than one might?). But I think that in the sphere of duties to self it may be natural to use the term 'ideals' to apply even to what are agreed to be duties, and think of them as duties to fulfil an ideal, as it were. This is partly because the duties concerned are duties to make something of oneself, to become a certain sort of person, rather than to adhere to certain rules, often rules about what *not* to do, as in the case of more conventional duties. These duties to oneself therefore possess a kind of creative quality. As such, moreover, they can present themselves as attractive as well as obligatory, and in this too are less like what I might call conventional duties.

It might still be said that duties to others are more *basic* than duties to oneself, in that the former preserve the fabric of society without which we could not cultivate ourselves. To a large extent this is true, as we saw in chapter 2 when discussing medicine. But even if 'the fabric of society' is in a state of collapse, there are *some* forms of *eudaemonia* which can still be sustained; moral virtue and friendship perhaps have their greatest opportunity in such situations. In any case, the fact that duties to others are necessary to enable us to pursue *eudaemonia* does not show that they are more important than the pursuit of *eudaemonia*. On the contrary, they might be construed, as I have suggested in chapter 2, as mere means to the end of the pursuit of *eudaemonia*.

What might be meant, however, is that the pursuit of *eudaemonia* is less *urgent* than, say, the relief of misery. It might be granted that *sub specie aeternitatis* scholarship, friendship and the contemplation of beauty are what are really important, but maintained that we must clear up the mess in the world a bit *first*, before we can get down to these things. Just as Plato's and Aristotle's philosophers had to win their leisure by a spell of public service, so (people might say) mankind at large must do so.

There is clearly something in this idea of the difference between urgency and importance (though I do not know how to analyse it, since both urgency and importance seem to imply preference in choice). But I suggest that it would be wrong to mortgage the present completely to the future in this matter, since who knows how far we shall ever be able to clear up the world? Even granted the urgency of relieving misery, therefore, we should make room for some leisure in the life of everyone, however useful he is, advocate the pursuit of *eudaemonia* in and through useful pursuits where possible, and allow some people of special gifts to preserve a thin stream of purer culture of mind and imagination wherewith to irrigate the rest.

There is still a difficulty in the idea of a duty to pursue *eudaemonia*: one concerned with *motive*. If something is a duty, presumably it can be, and on a Kantian view should be, performed out of a sense of duty. But there are some ingredients in *eudaemonia* which would, it seems, be destroyed if pursued out of a sense of duty. For example, appreciation of the arts or of other beauties is surely impossible, or at any rate loses its value, if performed out of a sense of duty. And to form friendships out of a sense of duty seems positively immoral – deceiving the people concerned and using them as a means.

Now this difficulty, although especially acute with regard to *eudaemonia*, concerns some duties to others too. For example, a mother has a duty to look after her children. But (*pace* Kant) it would seem unfortunate and inappropriate if she did this *out* of a sense of duty, at least in general. What happens, however, is that in general she will look after her children out of inclination, and duty comes into play only when inclination fails her – perhaps because of some distracting sorrow of her own.

Something similar can happen in the *eudaemonia* case. In general, people pursue the ingredients of *eudaemonia* out of inclination, and appropriately so. But a sense of duty might come in as a kind of supplement when inclination ran short. For example, a chronically shy person might need his sense of duty to get him to try to get to know people, though once he began to make acquaintances he should and probably will forget about duty and respond to the people as themselves. Again, an idle person might go to an art gallery or concert only out of a sense of duty, in the sense that mere inclination would never have got him there; but once there he might, rightly, forget about duty and simply enjoy himself. Again, a person might out of a sense of duty make the effort to begin a worthwhile but difficult book, but find that he becomes entirely captivated after a while and forgets duty altogether. These situations all seem to me commonplace. In none of them is the sense of duty so obtrusive as to destroy the good in question; one might rather see it as removing hinderances which prevent our natural inclinations from finding worthwhile outlets. But·clearly the pursuit of *eudaemonia* might become self-defeating if the sense of duty becomes *too* involved in it. What is needed, therefore, is some discernment on the part of the pursuer as to what he personally can come with a little effort to appreciate genuinely and spontaneously: a freedom from pretentiousness.

These considerations go some way towards answering the complaint that in my view there is no holiday from morality: every hour of the day one could be doing *something* improving, and even the pursuit of happiness has been removed from the sphere of the optional. It is true that I do not allow a holiday from morality, though there is in any case no reason why one should expect such a thing. But this does not mean that I hold that all the time one should be acting *out* of a sense of duty, or even thinking of duty. My view is that, as far as one's own life is concerned, dutifulness is only a *safety-net* motive to ensure that for duty's sake, if for no other, people should try to be happy and to find their happiness in a good life.

4   *Happiness*, Eudaemonia *and our Duties to Others*

I have assumed without argument that our duties to pursue happiness and *eudaemonia* for ourselves do not exhaust our duties, and that we also have duties to others. But it might be argued that our performance of duties to others can simply be *subsumed* under the pursuit of *eudaemonia* for ourselves. The life of moral obedience was earlier construed as constituting one form of *eudaemonia* by itself, though not the richest form; and certainly the dutiful performance of our duties to others is one ingredient in the kind of life we usually would want to call a case of *eudaemonia*. On this sort of view, we are urged to care for other people as part of the exercise of our own perfection.

This practice would normally be thought of as treating other people as means, and so wrong. But it should be noted that what is actually *done* would be the same whether it is done for the sake of others or for the sake of one's own perfection. So what is said to be wrong is not the actions themselves but acting thus from that motive – an instance of applying the notion of 'ought', or in this case 'ought not', to something other than a voluntary action. I would agree that it is unfitting to regard other people's welfare as necessarily subordinate in this way to one's own spiritual good; in that sense I disagree with what we may call egoistic ethical eudaemonism, and do not think that our only morally proper end is our own *eudaemonia*. But in saying this I am expressing a moral intuition about *motives*, not claiming that ethical egoistic eudaemonism does not do justice to our normal views on right *action* towards others, since a doctrine that we should act rightly towards others for our own sakes does not in itself lay down any particular view on what our duties to others are.

What, then, are we bound to do for others in respect of happiness and *eudaemonia*? I said earlier that we should promote others' *ends* rather than their happiness. But this is a choice only in a few cases. In very many cases, notably those where our duty is that of relieving misery, the two coincide, or may be presumed to do so. The choice arises, however, when people want us to permit or help with some project on which they are keen but which we think they will regret. Here I think the view would normally be taken that in general, where people have a right to expect help or co-operation, they do not forfeit it because their schemes are misconceived in the eyes of others. We do not necessarily assume they must know best – as I said in chapter 1, an onlooker may be a better judge than the person involved of what *will* make him happy, though not of whether he is happy now – but we assume they have a right to 'make their own mistakes'. Possible exceptions to this general principle would be children, who have some right to be *protected* against their own mistakes. To some degree governments also feel free to impose unpopular measures which they think will be in the public interest, presumably because they have been *deputed* to look after that interest to the best of their judgement.

This is only a sketch of an account of a topic which could occupy a whole book in itself. But even this sketch might be thought enough to show, by an *a fortiori* argument, that we can have no duties to promote others' *eudaemonia*. How, it may be asked, could it be thought other than patronising to try to 'improve' people, if even to give them what they will want rather than what they want now is to be frowned upon? Part of the answer lies in pointing out that some people actually want, perhaps not always very articulately but recognisably, to achieve *eudaemonia*. In these cases, we have the usual duties to promote other's ends, and especially (since negative duties, to avoid hindrance, are particularly stringent) to avoid getting in their way, mocking their efforts, and so on. This is not, however, a duty to promote their *eudaemonia* as such, but merely a duty to promote their ends.

Another part of the answer concerns the upbringing of children. It may be patronising to try to 'improve' adults, but it is not obviously patronising to try to improve children. I suggest that many of the tasks that parents and teachers see as incumbent upon them could be described as the promoting of the *eudaemonia* of their charges. Thus they say such things as that a child should learn when he is young to appreciate what is really beautiful or worthwhile, that he should make the most of himself and cultivate his talents, that he should develop the capacity for personal relationships, and so on; and they see their job as parents and teachers as involving the inculcation of these capacities. Of course this may be partly because they think the child is likely to be *happier* as a result. But I think that a child who turned out happy, but lacking in some of these capacities, would be regarded by many parents and teachers as a *failure* on their part; they would see their duty as the promotion of the child's true or real welfare, which would indeed include his happiness but would go beyond it. Moreover, they would hold that they can rightly coerce him to some extent to do things for the sake of his *eudaemonia*, just as they can for the sake of his future happiness.

In the case of adults, however, coercion in the name of *eudaemonia* is presumably ruled out, by a principle of liberty: those who have reached full age have a right to be a pig rather than a Socrates if they wish. It is ruled out even if we think Socrateses are happier than pigs, since as we saw we ought, in a case of conflict, to promote others' ends, however piglike, rather than their happiness. Some would add here that to coerce people in the name of *eudaemonia* is in any case self-defeating, but of that I am less sure. It is true that the exercise of free choice *might* be held to be a good in itself, and also that many goods in themselves are spoilt if pursued under coercion. But it might well be thought that a man who freely chooses to become a drug addict has lost *eudaemonia* for ever, whereas a man who is made to go to worthwhile plays and read worthwhile books *may* become keen on them for their own sakes.

But the question still arises whether we have any duty to promote *eudaemonia* in others by more indirect, non-coercive means: by preaching it, by private patronage of the arts, and so on. Even this might be thought patronising, until one considers what people often feel towards friends and others who are close to them. When people really care about someone, they often want, not merely to promote his happiness, but to make him in all respects the best he can be; and they may hold that they have a *duty* to criticise and advise their friends from this point of view. Indeed, to *refrain* from doing so might be patronising, implying the idea that lower standards than one's own are good enough for someone else. If really caring about someone naturally includes this concern for his true welfare or *eudaemonia*, ought we not to have some measure of this concern for everyone? Of course it will usually not be appropriate to express criticism except to friends.[10] But perhaps we have a duty, with regard to the *eudaemonia* as well as the happiness of others, to do such things as preserve the beauty of the environment; support schemes to take theatre or music to places which do not usually get them; encourage the improvement of public libraries whether or not we ourselves need them; patronise struggling artists, and so on.

Very often, of course, these tasks are carried out nowadays by the government rather than by individuals, and there is certainly a limit to what individuals can do. But government action in this sphere raises a problem. I said that it would be wrong to *coerce* people to go in for *eudaemonia*. But someone might object that in a sense the government does just that, since it extorts money from people who are not interested in culture at all and uses it to subsidise the arts and scholarship. I think this practice would be hard to defend from a purely hedonistic-utilitarian point of view, even taking into account the fact that what the government supports in this way, although a minority interest, at any given time, is often a perennial one. But perhaps one might defend the practice, and incidentally lend further support to the view that there is a duty to further others' *eudaemonia*, by suggesting that a government is held to be to some extent empowered, not only to look after our interests as it sees fit, but also to carry out those of our *moral duties* which (whether or not we acknowledge them) it holds to be both incumbent on members of the community and best carried out by government action; and successive governments have put into this category the duty of fostering the *eudaemonia* of others.[11]

5 Conclusions

In this essay I have argued that happiness in our normal modern sense of the word is an attitude to our lives which *can* be pursued but is not *necessarily* pursued, either as a sole end or as one among several ends, or even necessarily wanted by everyone. I have articulated a concept of *eudaemonia*, as the life which is worth living or good in itself, and some possible criteria for deciding what can form the ingredients of such a life. I have explored the relationships between this *eudaemonia* and hedonistic happiness, and concluded that, whereas *eudaemonia* is empirically neither necessary nor sufficient for happiness, happiness might be part of the definition of *eudaemonia* and so a logically necessary condition of it; and also that the pursuit of *eudaemonia* is a quite reasonable policy to adopt in pursuing happiness. Finally, I considered whether, and if so in what sense, we ought to pursue either happiness or *eudaemonia*. I concluded that there is a kind of hypothetical imperative enjoining the pursuit of happiness, and hence of *eudaemonia*, if that is the best means to happiness; that we have a *prima facie* duty to pursue happiness, if it can be regarded as required for personal integratedness, or its pursuit as an exercise in the distinctive human endowment of rationality; that we have a *prima facie* duty to pursue *eudaemonia* for ourselves; that in general we have a duty to promote others' ends and (in non-coercive ways) their *eudaemonia*.

In what sense then is happiness, whether our ordinary hedonistic happiness or *eudaemonia*, the proper or appropriate end for man? It is prudentially and morally appropriate for him to seek happiness, especially through *eudaemonia*, where only he is concerned; but happiness cannot be regarded as *the* morally appropriate end, if this means that a man should seek his own happiness without regard to that of others. It might be thought that I still could hold that happiness is *the* end for man, in the universalised sense: mankind in general should seek the *general* happiness and it alone. But I am doubtful about this view, even if 'happiness' includes *eudaemonia*. That is to say, I think we should normally hold that there are some duties which, even if they can be construed as the promotion of some goods, are not duties to produce *happiness* in any sense. The duty of justice, for example, though it can if one wishes be depicted teleologically as the duty to bring about a just order or just distribution, is not a duty to bring about happiness as such, even though it may be that what the distribution is a distribution *of* is happiness. Again, I have hinted earlier that the goods in themselves, the ingredients which make a life good, might be seen as having a claim on us which logically could cut across the claims of both a maximum and a just distribution of happiness, whether hedonistic happiness or *eudaemonia*. If these points are sound, there is no sense in which happiness is *the* appropriate end for man.

References

1 *The Nature of Happiness*

1. The discussion in this section owes much to Roger Montague, 'Happiness', *Proceedings of the Aristotelian Society*, vol. LXVII (1966–7) and D. A. Lloyd Thomas, 'Happiness', *Philosophical Quarterly*, vol. 18 (1968).

2. Aristotle, *Nicomachean Ethics*, 1095b, 15.

3. See R. M. Hare, *Freedom and Reason* (Oxford University Press, 1963) pp. 127–8.

4. Aristotle, *Nicomachean Ethics*, 1100a, 10.

5. Gilbert Ryle, 'Pleasure', *Proceedings of the Aristotelian Society, Supplementary Volume* 28 (1954).

6. John Stuart Mill, *Utilitarianism*, ed. Mary Warnock (Collins, The Fontana Library, 1962) ch. IV.

7. Aristotle, *Nicomachean Ethics*, 1094a, 1–3, 18–22; 1095a, 14–20.

8. Aristotle, *Eudemian Ethics*, A2, 1214b, 6–14.

9. Aristotle, *Nicomachean Ethics*, 1095b, 14–1096a, 10; 1113a, 15–1113b, 2.

10. See Anthony Kenny, 'Happiness', *Proceedings of the Aristotelian Society* vol. LXVI (1965–6).

11. See, for example, Anthony Kenny, *Action, Emotion and Will* (Routledge, 1963) p. 146.

2 Eudaemonia

1. See for example Plato, *Republic*, 580d–588a; Aristotle, *Nicomachean Ethics*, 1178a, 4–8.

2. Aldous Huxley, *Brave New World* (Chatto & Windus, 1932).

3. For example, P. T. Geach, in 'Good And Evil', *Analysis* vol. 17 (1956).

4. W. D. Ross, *Foundations of Ethics* (Oxford, 1939) pp. 257–8.

5. See G. E. M. Anscombe, *Intention* (Basil Blackwell, 1958) pp. 69–71.

6. See R. S. Downie and Elizabeth Telfer, *Respect for Persons* (George Allen & Unwin, 1969) pp. 13–15.

7. Aristotle, *Metaphysics*, 1048b, 18–35.

8. See W. F. R. Hardie, *Aristotle's Ethical Theory* (Oxford University Press, 1968) pp. 13–14, 306.

9. Aristotle, *Nicomachean Ethics*, 1095b, 29–1096a, 2; 1098b, 30–1099a, 2.

10. George Herbert, 'The Elixir'.

11. See R. S. Peters, *Ethics and Education* (George Allen & Unwin, 1966) pp. 156, 175–8.

12. Aristotle, *Nicomachean Ethics*, 1097b, 22–1098a, 18.

13. Kant, *Groundwork of the Metaphysic of Morals*, trans. H. J. Paton as *The Moral Law* (Hutchinson's University Library, 1948) p. 61.

14. Aristotle, *Nicomachean Ethics*, 1099a, 31–b2; 1155a, 7–9, 1177a, 28–32.

15. Kant, *Groundwork*, p. 62.

16. See W. D. Hudson, *Modern Moral Philosophy* (Macmillan, 1970) pp. 274–5.

17. On this point, see W. G. Maclagan, 'How Important Is Moral Goodness?', *Mind* vol. 64 (1965).

18. This example was suggested by G. E. M. Anscombe, 'Thought And Action In Aristotle', in *New Essays on Plato and Aristotle*, ed. Renford Bambrough (Routledge & Kegan Paul, 1965) p. 149.

19. John Stuart Mill, *Utilitarianism*, ed. Mary Warnock (Collins, The Fontana Library, 1962) pp. 254–5.

20. See G. E. Moore, *Principia Ethica* (Cambridge University Press, 1903) pp. ix–x.

21. Moore, *Principia Ethica*, p. 189.

22. For this 'proof' see John Stuart Mill, *Utilitarianism*, ed. Mary Warnock (Collins, The Fontana Library, 1962) ch. IV.

23. For his general account of his method of argument see Peters, *Ethics and Education*, pp. 114–16.

24. Ibid., p. 164.

25. Downie and Telfer, *Respect for Persons*, pp. 153–5.

26. J. N. Findlay, *Axiological Ethics* (Macmillan, 1970).

27. Ibid., p. 83.

28. Ibid., p. 84.

29. Ibid., p. 87.

30. Ibid.

31. Ibid.

32. John Stuart Mill, *On Liberty*, ed. Mary Warnock (Collins, The Fontana Library, 1962) p. 187.

33. Ibid., p. 136.

34. See R. S. Downie, 'Mill on Pleasure and Self-Development', *Philosophical Quarterly* vol. 16 (1966).

35. Kant, *Groundwork*, pp. 97–8.

36. Mill, *On Liberty*, pp. 191–2.

37. Aristotle, *Nicomachean Ethics*, 1097b, 22–1098a, 18.

38. Ibid., 1097b, 22–1098a, 18; 1102a, 5–1103a, 10.

39. Ibid., 1098a, 16–18.

40. Ibid., 1097a, 25–b5; 1176a, 30–b7.

41. Ibid., 1176a, 30–1179a, 32.

42. Ibid., 1178b, 5–6.

43. Ibid., 1177b, 6–7.

44. Ibid., 1178a, 9–10.

45. Ibid., 1144a, 1–6.

46. Mill, *On Liberty*, p. 187.

47. Aristotle, *Nicomachean Ethics*, 1176b, 33–5.

48. Aristotle, *De Poetica*, 1449b, 26.

49. I return to this point in chapter 3, section 4.

50. Aristotle, *Nicomachean Ethics*, books VIII and IX.

51. Ibid., 1156b, 6–24.

52. On friendship, see W. G. Maclagan, 'Respect for Persons as a Moral Principle', *Philosophy* vol. XXXV (1960); Elizabeth Telfer, 'Friendship', *Proceedings of the Aristotelian Society* vol. LXXI (1970–1).

53. Plato, *Republic*, 392c, 6–398b, 8.

54. For a discussion of Aristotle's views in terms of self-realisation, see John Hospers, *Human Conduct* (Hart-Davis, 1970) pp. 79–90.

55. This is implied by Mill, *On Liberty*, p. 187.

3   *The Relation between* Eudaemonia *and Hedonistic Happiness*

1. R. S. Peters, *Ethics And Education* (Allen & Unwin, 1966) ch. V *et passim*.

2. John Stuart Mill, *Utilitarianism*, ed. Mary Warnock (Collins, The Fontana Library, 1962) pp. 259–60.

3. See Peters, *Ethics and Education*, pp. 155–6.

4. Aristotle, *Nicomachean Ethics*, 1153a, 12–15; cf. 1174b, 14–1175a, 3.

5. Ibid., 1099a, 18–20; 1104b, 3–9.

6. Kant, *Groundwork of the Metaphysics of Morals*, trans. H. J. Paton as *The Moral Law* (Hutchinson's University Library, 1948) p. 66.

7. Aristotle, *Nicomachean Ethics*, 1117b, 7–16.

8. See I. M. Crombie, *An Examination of Plato's Doctrines* (Routledge & Kegan Paul, 1962) vol. I, pp. 265–9.

9. Aristotle, *Nicomachean Ethics*, 1175b, 24–9.

10. See A. C. Ewing, *Teach Yourself Ethics* (English Universities Press, 1953) p. 45.

11. Compare Aristotle, *Nicomachean Ethics*, 1173b, 25–8.

12. W. D. Ross, *Foundations of Ethics* (Oxford University Press, 1939) pp. 271–89.

13. Aristotle, *Nicomachean Ethics*, 1177b, 4–6.

14. Ibid., 1176b, 9–1177a, 11.

15. For discussions of the aesthetic aspect of games, see for example Harold Osborne, 'Notes on the Aesthetics of Chess and the Concept of Intellectual Beauty', *British Journal of Aesthetics* vol. 4 (1964); C. L. James, *Beyond A Boundary* (Hutchinson, 1963).

16. John Stuart Mill, *On Liberty*, ed. Mary Warnock (Collins, The Fontana Library, 1962) pp. 188–90, 193–4, 199–200.

17. C. L. Stevenson, 'The Emotive Meaning of Ethical Terms', *Mind* vol. 46 (1937).

18. See C. A. Campbell, 'Ethics Without Propositions', *Mind* vol. 59 (1950).

19. See Peters, *Ethics and Education*, p. 154.

4   *Happiness as the End of Life*

1. The most famous challenge is that of Joseph Butler, *Sermon XI*, section 20, from *Sermons* edited by W. R. Matthews (G. Bell and Sons, 1964). See also

Henry Sidgwick, *The Methods of Ethics* (Macmillan, seventh edn repr. 1963) pp. 506–9.

2. Kant, *Groundwork of the Metaphysic of Morals*, trans. by H. J. Paton as *The Moral Law* (Hutchinson's University Library, 1948) p. 85.

3. Compare Bernard Williams, *Morality* (Penguin, 1972) pp. 92–5.

4. Kant, *Groundwork*, p. 67.

5. For the idea of the asymmetry of morality, see W. G. Maclagan, 'Self And Others: A Defence Of Altruism', *Philosophical Quarterly* vol. 4 (1954).

6. For the distinction between rights of action and rights of recipience, see D. D. Raphael, 'Human Rights', *Proceedings of the Aristotelian Society, Supplementary Volume* XXXIX (1965).

7. John Stuart Mill, *On Liberty*, ed. Mary Warnock (Collins, The Fontana Library, 1962) p. 135.

8. John Stuart Mill, *Utilitarianism*, ed. Mary Warnock (Collins, The Fontana Library, 1962) p. 304.

9. For the notion of supererogatory actions see J. O. Urmson, 'Saints and Heroes', *Essays in Moral Philosophy* ed. A. I. Melden (University of Washington Press, 1958).

10. See R. S. Downie, 'The Right to Criticise', *Philosophy* vol. XLIV (1969).

11. For the notion of the government as a moral intermediary, see R. S. Downie, *Government Action And Morality* (Macmillan, 1964) ch. V.

Index